Practical Guide
For Private
Investigators

Practical Guide
For Private
Investigators

Edward Smith

PALADIN PRESS
BOULDER, COLORADO

Practical Guide for Private Investigators
by Edward R. Smith

Copyright © 1982, 1990 by Edward R. Smith
First Edition: ISBN 0-87364-255-4
Second Edition: ISBN 0-87364-553-7
Printed in the United States of America

Published by Paladin Press, a division of
Paladin Enterprises, Inc., P.O. Box 1307,
Boulder, Colorado 80306, USA.
(303) 443-7250

Direct inquiries and/or orders to the above address.

Table of Contents

Foreword. vii
Introduction. 1
1. Private Detectives and the Law. 3
2. Criminal and Civil Law. 12
3. The Law of Evidence. 18
4. Criminal Investigation. 29
5. Physical or Real Evidence. 37
6. Developing Leads. 44
7. Interviews and Interrogation. 55
8. Surveillance. 65
9. Homicide Investigation. 72
10. Arson Investigation. 78
11. Other Criminal Investigations. 85
12. Divorce Investigation. 96
13. Other Civil Investigations. 106
14. Starting Your Own Business. 112

Glossary. 117
Final Examinations. 124

Foreword

Proficiency in the art of private investigation is achieved through a combination of technical course study and practical experience. My purpose in writing this book is to impart basic knowledge and skills to the reader so that he can obtain entry-level employment as a private detective, store detective, or an undercover operative. Only after attaining an entry-level position can practical experience be gained.

I have devoted my life to the study and practice of law enforcement and private investigations. Because of my formal college education, investigative training, and experience, I feel that I am well qualified to present this subject to the layman who has not had any practical experience.

Many references will be made in this book to various criminal laws. I tried to present general definitions of criminal laws so that the reader will be able to grasp the basic concepts of law. Within the United States, marked variations occur from one state to another in both the language and content of criminal laws so that no uniform set of state criminal laws exists in this country.

In closing, I should add that the key to success here is hard work. I have made it easier for the reader to learn the basics of the private detective profession by preparing this book. It instructs the reader as to how an investigation should be carried out. Remember, the field of private investigation is not easy. But through hard work, you will find that the profession is a truly rewarding one.

E.R.S.

Introduction

The private detective profession is highly skilled and challenging. It is not possible to become a successful private detective merely by reading about it. A person must also have practical experience. It can be compared to becoming a piano player. To become a piano player, one does not only read about music theory; one must actually practice on the piano. This practice is also called experience.

The profession is no longer limited to men. Females also have the same opportunities as do the men. The opportunities for both men and women are numerous. The following is a list of businesses that may utilize the services of a private detective and the type of services the private detective will be performing:

Law firms—claims investigations, divorce investigations, locating missing persons, criminal investigations.

Banks—credit investigations, background investigations.

Department stores—undercover investigations, credit investigations, background investigations, criminal investigations.

Food stores—criminal investigations, background investigations, credit investigations, undercover investigations.

Industrial—undercover investigations, criminal investigations, background investigations.

Insurance companies—background investigations, criminal investigations, claims investigations.

Detective agencies—any type of investigation mentioned above.

The private detective profession is not a nine to five occupation. A private detective must be prepared to work long and hard hours, as well as working at night and on weekends. In spite of these facts, the occupation does not go unrewarded. The private detective will enjoy prestige, excitement, personal satisfaction, and financial reward.

Each state regulates the private detective profession in different ways. A listing contained in this book provides the reader with the basic requirements that each state has set down. The best rule to follow when starting up a private detective business is to research the laws in your state. There are stiff penalties if one does not adhere to the letter of the law.

The chapters that discuss specific criminal offenses are presented in such a manner that the reader will get a basic understanding of the various criminal offenses and investigative steps needed to complete the investigation. It is impossible to discuss criminal offenses in great detail because of the marked variations that occur from one state to another in the content and language of criminal offenses. Because of this, the private detective must research the criminal law that governs his state. If a question on law arises, an attorney should be consulted.

Civil investigations will also be conducted by the private detective. Civil investigations differ from criminal investigations only in the subject matter being investigated and the law that applies to the matter at hand. The basic procedures for investigation that are presented in this book apply to both civil and criminal investigations.

All investigations should be objective, thorough, relevant, and accurate. They must also answer the questions: "Who?" "What?" "Where?" "When?" "Why?" and "How?"

It is obviously important for the private detective to be regarded as dependable, honest, and trustworthy. While acting in his professional capacity, the private detective should abide by the following five principles:

1. Perform investigations in a professional, moral, and ethical manner.
2. Work within the framework of the law.
3. Conduct investigations in a lawful manner.
4. Protect confidential information.
5. Tell the whole truth when presenting evidence.

If the reader absorbs the information contained in this book and follows the basic principles of conduct, he will be well on his way to becoming a professional investigator.

1. Private Detectives and the Law

In practically all states, a private detective has the equivalent powers of a private citizen to make arrests, to defend himself and others, to investigate, and to carry firearms. Some states have specific laws which govern the performance of private detectives. Again, before setting up a business, research the law and consult your attorney.

Arrest/False Arrest

An arrest occurs when an individual is lawfully deprived of his personal freedom. Detaining a person can be classified as an arrest, and one may be liable for false arrest if the arresting detective is wrong.

A private detective generally has the right to protect the safety of the public and can arrest for an act constituting a breach of peace. The best rule of thumb is: If you know for a fact (i.e., you saw the crime being committed) that a crime has been committed, then and only then should you make an arrest. If you live by this rule, you will never be charged with false arrest or sued in civil court.

Search and Seizure

A search is an examination of a person's house or other buildings, or of his person, in order to discover evidence of guilt to be used in a court of law.

There are three basic instances in which a detective can search legally:

- Actual consent by the suspect.
- Incidental to a valid arrest.
- Implied consent (as a condition to employment).

3

Many states have laws which forbid the detective from doing some or all of the above. Again, check with your attorney. If during your legal search you find contraband, it is legal to seize it.

Use of Force

When a private detective reasonably believes that some person intends to do him harm, he can use reasonable force to repel the attack. The detective may also use force to repel an attack on the safety and lives of others. Again, the force must be reasonable.

The private detective may use deadly force only when the following conditions are met:

- When he reasonably believes he is in danger of serious bodily injury or death.
- When he reasonably believes that someone else is in danger of serious bodily injury or death.
- When he has retreated to a reasonable end (he retreated to the wall and had no place to go).

Remember, deadly force is never sanctioned for the defense of property. Property can be replaced, but a human life cannot.

Defamation of Character

Defamation of character is damage done to the reputation of a person. This is why the private detective should make a thorough investigation and be sure that all the facts are true. If he is wrong, the character of a person could be injured, and the private detective could be sued in civil court for damages.

The private detective should never use defamatory words and never prejudge a person. If the private detective communicates these points to another, defamation takes place. Remember that defamation can take the form of speech (slander) or written form (libel).

The paramount rule here is: always work within the law. If you have any questions regarding the law, consult your attorney.

Private Detective Regulation

When setting up a private detective business, the potential private detective must consider the licensing regulations that govern this field. They vary from state to state but are basically the same. A majority of the states have adopted licensing regulations that a private detective applicant must be able to meet. Since laws are continuously changing, it is best to check with your state government. A state-by-state listing of these regulations follows.

Alabama

No regulation for the private detective industry.

Alaska

No regulation for the private detective industry.

Arizona

An applicant must be a U.S. citizen, twenty-one years of age or older, free of felony convictions, and a person of good character. An applicant must have one to three years of related experience.

Arkansas

An applicant must be a U.S. citizen, twenty-two years of age or older, of good character, and have no felony convictions. An applicant must have two years of related experience.

California

An applicant must be a U.S. citizen, twenty-one years of age or older, of good character, and have no felony convictions. An applicant must also have two years of related experience.

Colorado

An applicant must be eighteen years of age or older, have no felony convictions, and be of good character. An applicant must also have two years of related experience.

Connecticut

An applicant must be a U.S. citizen, twenty years of age or older, of good character, and have no felony convictions. An applicant must also have five years of related experience.

Delaware

An applicant must be a U.S. citizen, have a clean criminal record, and be of good character.

Florida

An applicant must be a U.S. citizen, be twenty-one years of age or older, have no felony convictions, be of good character, and have one to two years of related experience.

Georgia

An applicant must be a U.S. citizen, be twenty-one years of age or older, have no felony convictions, and be of good character. An applicant must also have two years of related experience.

Hawaii

An applicant must be a U.S. citizen, be twenty-five years of age or older, have no felony convictions, and be of good character. An applicant must also have four years of related experience.

Idaho

No regulation for the private detective industry.

Illinois

An applicant must be a U.S. citizen, be twenty-one years of age or older, have no felony convictions, and be of good character. An applicant must also have three years of related experience.

Indiana

An applicant must be a U.S. citizen, be twenty-one years of age or older, have no felony convictions, and be of good character. An applicant must also have two years of related experience.

Iowa

An applicant must be a U.S. citizen, be eighteen years of age or older, have no felony convictions, and be of good character.

Kansas

An applicant must be a U.S. citizen, be twenty-two years of age or older, have no felony convictions, and be of good character.

Kentucky

No regulation for the private detective industry.

Louisiana

No regulation for the private detective industry.

Maine

An applicant must be a U.S. citizen, be twenty-one years of age or older, have no felony convictions, and be of good character. An applicant must also have one year of related experience.

Maryland

An applicant must be a U.S. citizen, have no felony convictions, be twenty-five years of age or older, and be of good character. An applicant must also have three years of related experience.

Massachusetts

An applicant must be a U.S. citizen, be twenty-five years of age or older, have no felony convictions, and be of good character. An applicant must also have three years of related experience.

Michigan

An applicant must be a U.S. citizen, be twenty-five years of age or older, have no felony convictions, and be of good character. An applicant must also have two years of related experience.

Minnesota

An applicant must be a U.S. citizen, be twenty-one years of age or older, have no felony convictions, and be of good character. An applicant must also have three years of related experience.

Mississippi

No regulation for the private detective industry.

Missouri

No regulation for the private detective industry.

Montana

An applicant must be a U.S. citizen, be twenty-one years of age or older, have no felony convictions, and be of good character. An applicant must also have three years of related experience.

Nebraska

An applicant must be a U.S. citizen, be twenty-two years of age or older, have no felony convictions, and be of good character.

Nevada

An applicant must be a U.S. citizen, be twenty-one years of age or older, have no felony convictions, and be of good character.

New Hampshire

An applicant must be eighteen years of age or older, have no felony convictions, and be of good character.

New Jersey

An applicant must be a U.S. citizen, be twenty-five years of age or older, have no felony convictions, and be of good character. An applicant must also have five years of related experience.

New Mexico

An applicant must be a U.S. citizen, be twenty-one years of age or older, have no felony convictions, and be of good character. An applicant must also have at least two years of related experience.

New York

An applicant must be a U.S. citizen, be twenty-five years of age or older, have no felony convictions, and be of good character. An applicant must also have three years of related experience.

North Carolina

An applicant must be a U.S. citizen, be twenty-one years of age or older, have no felony convictions, and be of good character. An applicant must also have three years of related experience.

North Dakota

An applicant must be a U.S. citizen, be twenty-one years of age or older, have no felony convictions, and be of good character.

Ohio

An applicant must be a U.S. citizen, have no felony convictions, and be of good character. An applicant must also have two years of related experience.

Oklahoma

No regulation for the private detective industry.

Oregon

No regulation for the private detective industry.

Pennsylvania

An applicant must be a U.S. citizen, be twenty-five years of age or older, have no felony convictions, and be of good character. An applicant must have three years of related experience.

Rhode Island

An applicant must be a U.S. citizen, have no felony convictions, and be of good character.

South Carolina

An applicant must be a U.S. citizen, be twenty-one years of age or older, have no felony convictions, and be of good character. An applicant must also have two years of related experience.

South Dakota

No regulation for the private detective industry.

Tennessee

No regulation for the private detective industry.

Texas

An applicant must be a U.S. citizen, be twenty-one years of age or older, have no felony convictions, and be of good character. An applicant must also have two years of related experience.

Utah

No regulation for the private detective industry.

Vermont

An applicant must be twenty-one years of age or older, have no felony convictions, and be of good character. An applicant must also have two years of related experience.

Virginia

An applicant must be twenty-one years of age or older, have no felony convictions, and be of good character.

Washington

No regulation for the private detective industry.

West Virginia

An applicant must be a U.S. citizen, be twenty-one years of age or older, have no felony convictions, and be of good character. An applicant must have three years of related experience.

Wisconsin

An applicant must be eighteen years of age or older, have no felony convictions, and be of good character. An applicant must have three years of related experience.

Wyoming

No regulation for the private detective industry.

REVIEW QUESTIONS

1. What is the definition of an arrest?
2. What are the basic instances in which a private detective can make a legal search?
3. Under what conditions may deadly force be used?
4. What is meant by defamation of character?
5. What are some of the requirements that state law places upon a private detective applicant?

2. Criminal and Civil Law

A set of enforced rules under which a society is governed is the definition of law. Without law, no society could exist. Law establishes the rules that define a person's rights, a person's obligations to the rights of others, the penalties for persons who violate these rules, and the procedures on how the government shall enforce the rules and penalties. Law can be divided into two branches: public and private. Public law concerns the rights and obligations people have to society. Criminal law is a branch of public law. Private law, which is also called civil law, concerns the rights and obligations people have to one another.

In a large nation such as ours, variations of law exist from one state to another in both the content and language of criminal and civil laws. It is important for the private detective to keep this in mind. Always check the laws that govern your state.

Criminal Law

Criminal law deals with crimes. A crime is an act or omission forbidden by law. It is a violation of a public law. Crimes are sorted into felonies and misdemeanors. Felonies are those crimes thought to be most serious and heinous, and carry maximum penalties of death or imprisonment. Misdemeanors, on the other hand, are regarded as relatively petty acts of lesser significance. They are usually punishable by fines. Although criminal codes in all of the states distinguish between the two categories of offense, the felony-misdemeanor distinctions are not uniform from one state to another. In one state, the felony of grand larceny involves theft of goods valued over $500, while in another state grand larceny is

12

defined as any theft of goods valued over $250. Accordingly, behavior which is a misdemeanor in one state is a felony in another.

Elements of Crime

There must be two elements present in any crime; criminal intent and a criminal act. The law, in effect, says we will not punish a man if he merely intends to commit a crime and does not act toward its accomplishment, nor will the law punish a man if he commits an unlawful act accidentally. But if he does act and has the criminal intent, then he is liable to punishment. Consequently, we may lay down the general rule that to constitute a crime there must be an act and an intent.

Criminal Intent

Intent is that mental element which directs some unlawful act. Motive is the reason a man does an unlawful act. Intent is an essential element for crime. Motive is not. Motive, however, is important as evidence of intent. It helps to prove the identity of the person, the act, or the intent. It makes little difference what the motive is in determining a person's guilt or innocence.

Specific intent is that kind of criminal intent which is particular in nature. Murder, burglary, robbery, and theft are just a few crimes that require specific intent. It is important to know the particular law in question because some crimes require specific intent while others do not. Violations of the pure food laws and liquor laws, for example, do not require specific intent. The laws were written so that such negligence is declared to be a crime even though no intent exists.

Gross negligence, recklessness, carelessness, or disregard of the material consequences of an act can take the place of specific intent. Thus, strictly speaking, this is another exception to the general rule that every crime requires an act and an intent. But to do justice the law says that in these cases the gross negligence takes the place of the intent.

If the defendant was insane at the time of the commission of the offense, he has a complete defense, the reason being that the insane person was incapable of forming criminal intent. Since early common law, society always has been careful to protect one who is insane. An insane person is considered a ward of the state. Since he is not capable of forming a criminal intent, the law does not choose to punish him. The test generally used to determine sanity is whether or not the person can distinguish the difference between right and wrong, or the nature and quality of the act constituting the crime. A person may have been sane when he committed the crime and insane at the time of the trial. In that event, he cannot be tried since he is not capable of defending himself. The court will protect him by committing him to an institution. If and when he becomes sane, he may then be tried.

Generally, children under the age of seven are presumed to be incapable of forming a criminal intent. A child between the ages of seven and twelve is still considered incapable of forming a criminal intent. But if the prosecution can prove that the child had the mental capacity to know the nature of the act that he committed and to know it was wrong, then the child can be held accountable for his actions. A child between the ages of twelve and sixteen is presumed to be capable of forming criminal intent. Jurisdiction over such persons who are presumed to be capable of forming criminal intent is given to juvenile courts where they are tried not for the specific crime but for juvenile delinquency. However, when an act which, if committed by an adult, would be punishable with death or life imprisonment, is committed by the juvenile, then the juvenile may be tried as an adult. Murder is a good example of this type of crime.

Duress is when a person is forced or compelled to do a criminal act by another. It cannot be said that such a person formed criminal intent. The act was not his will but that of another. Therefore, the law absolves him from the crime. The duress must be immediate and continuous throughout the act, so as to produce a well-grounded apprehension of death or serious bodily harm. Duress, however, does not permit a person to take the life of an innocent third person to save his own.

Voluntary intoxication is no defense to a crime except where actual intent is an essential element of the crime, as in first degree murder, larceny, forgery, bribery, etcetera. In such cases, if the defendant is so intoxicated that he cannot form the actual intent, he is not capable of committing the crime. Involuntary intoxication is a defense, but the situation is rare.

Ignorance of the law excuses no one. Such is the general rule as to the mistake of law. Thus, it is no defense for larceny to say that you did not know it was against the law to steal. However, in some cases, mistake of law is a good defense where the act is prohibited by statute and the law with respect to that act is not settled or plain. A mistake of fact where it is honest, bona fide, and reasonable, will negate the intent and be a defense in certain circumstances. The mistake must be such that, had the circumstances been as the defendant thought they were, no guilt would have attached. Also, the mistake must be reasonable. Both tests must apply.

There are certain crimes which by their very nature a corporation cannot commit, such as murder, larceny, burglary, and so on. There are others, such as obtaining money by false pretenses, mailing obscene matter, and nuisance, which it can commit. So far as punishment is concerned, a corporation may be fined but obviously not imprisoned.

Criminal Act

There can be no crime unless a person commits some unlawful act. The law does not punish a man for his intentions, no matter how evil they may be. The criminal act and the criminal intent must both occur. It is sufficient if the intent is present at the time of the act. It need not be present any special length of time.

Many states have passed a law making it a crime to ask another to commit a crime even though the crime was not committed. It is held that the solicitation itself constitutes the criminal act and the ultimate crime solicited need not occur.

States have also passed a law where an agreement between two or more persons to do an unlawful act in an unlawful manner is a crime. The essence of this crime, called conspiracy, is the agreement. That agreement constitutes the criminal act.

An attempt to commit a crime has been held by many states as a crime in itself. An attempt is an act done beyond mere preparation, with intent to commit it, but falling short of its actual commission. There must be an overt act directly moving toward its commission. The overt act must be such as will apparently result in a crime if not hindered by extraneous causes in the commission of the crime itself. Thus, there are two main elements in this crime: an intent to commit the crime, and a direct ineffectual act done toward its commission. For example, a person enters a department store and notices that the sales person has left a display of watches out on the counter. The subject takes one watch out of the display but before he can get the watch into his pocket, the watch falls out of his hand. The subject then runs out of the store and the watch is left lying on the floor.

Civil Law

Civil law defines the rights and obligations people have in their relations with one another. The majority of judges and lawyers spend most of their time working with civil law matters. Some of these cases, called lawsuits, are settled out of court while others go to court where a judge and jury must decide if a person's civil law rights have been violated.

Civil law can be generally divided into six categories: tort law, family law, commercial/contract law, corporation law, inheritance law, and property law.

Tort law is concerned mainly with injuries to persons, reputations, and personal property. A tort is a private wrong. The affected party has the right to collect money to pay for damages suffered.

Family law governs the obligation and rights of wives and husbands and of parents and children.

Commercial/contract law deals with the obligations and rights of persons who make contracts.

Property law is concerned with the use and the ownership of property whether real (land or building) or personal (car, boat, etc.).

Corporation law deals with the formation and operation of corporations.

Inheritance law governs the transfer of property based upon the owner's death.

The private detective will be involved in civil investigations. A majority of his cases will come from the following categories of civil law:

Tort law investigations—accidents, defamation of character, negligence, personal injury, assault, and false arrest, are all examples of cases that a private detective can investigate.

Family law investigations—divorce, locating missing spouses, and locating missing children, are all examples of cases that a private detective can investigate.

Commercial/contract law investigations—locating missing debtors, contract fraud, and insurance contract claims are all examples of cases that a private detective can investigate.

REVIEW QUESTIONS

1. What is meant by the term *law*?
2. What are the two branches of law? Discuss both branches.
3. What are the two elements of a crime? Distinguish between the two elements.
4. What is intent? Does every crime need the element of intent?
5. What are the six categories of civil law?

3. The Law of Evidence

Evidence is that which demonstrates, makes clear, or ascertains the truth of the very fact or point in issue, either on one side or the other. It supplies proof. A successful investigation depends largely on the private detective's skill in the recognition, evaluation, and collection of evidence and upon his understanding of the fundamental rules governing the admission and rejection of evidence.

Admissibility of Evidence

Tests of admissibility are applied to all evidence. Unless the evidence meets those tests, it cannot be introduced in a court of law. There are three principal tests of admissibility that must be met before testimony or physical evidence is allowed into evidence: relevancy, materiality, and competency.

Relevancy concerns the logical relation between the proposed evidence and a fact to be proved. Evidence which tends to establish a fact at issue is relevant. If it does not tend to prove either the truth or probability, or the untruth or improbability of the fact at issue before the court, the evidence is irrelevant. Not all relevant evidence will be admitted simply because it is relevant. The trial judge must keep a trial within reasonable bounds, both as to the amount of time taken and the facts covered. If the court admitted all evidence, however slight and inconsequential, the trial might go on for years. For this reason, the court frowns upon any evidence which is only remotely connected with the case.

Material evidence is that evidence which bears on the credibility of the evidence in some supporting way. The evidence should properly influence the jury and/or judge to make a decision. Evidence is only material when it affects a fact or issue significantly.

18

Any event that is remote or inconsequential would not be material to an issue, and would be objectionable for that reason.

Competent evidence concerns evidence which is qualified, reliable, and suitable for the case in point. The test of competency applies to all evidence, but is most frequently encountered only with witnesses. A witness is competent if he knows right from wrong, knows the meaning of an oath, comprehends his obligation to tell the truth, and is able to observe, retain, and tell coherently what he observed. If an objection is made to the competency of a witness, this question is primarily determined by the court.

Burden of Proof

Proof is the result or effect of evidence. No person can be convicted of a crime unless the prosecution presents the evidence that is necessary for a conviction. In every criminal case, every fact essential to constitute the crime charged must be proven. Thus, the burden of proof is solely the responsibility of the prosecution.

In every criminal case, the prosecution must prove three facts in order to convict a person: the act charged was done or omitted, it was done by criminal means, and it was done by the accused. The proof must always be beyond a reasonable doubt.

Direct Evidence

Direct evidence is that means of proof which tends to show the existence of a fact in question without the intervention of proof of any other fact. It is derived from personal knowledge, in most cases from actually witnessing the event. When a witness testifies that he "heard a shot and saw the defendant running," he is giving direct evidence.

Circumstantial Evidence

Circumstantial or *indirect evidence* is that which tends to establish the issue by proof of various facts, sustaining by their consistency the hypothesis claimed. Circumstantial evidence may be described as the opposite of direct evidence. The essence of circumstantial evidence is inference, which draws a conclusion from facts or propositions known to be true.

While circumstantial evidence can lead to conclusions as strong as those arising from direct or real evidence, it never quite attains the level of these classifications. Accordingly, the wise private detective examines circumstantial evidence with the utmost caution and leaves no stone unturned in obtaining all the evidence he possibly can. Every witness who can shed light on the case should be sought and interrogated if at all possible because of the importance that direct evidence has in the courtroom. Further, the most painstaking effort should be made to obtain all real evidence because of its reliability and accuracy. Finally, every shred of circumstantial evidence should be carefully examined.

Long experience in court trials has shown that conviction or acquittal may hinge upon the care with which circumstantial facts and conduct are investigated and the way the evidence is submitted to the prosecution. Motive, intent, physical capacity to commit the act charged, skill or technical knowledge possessed by the accused, means or lack of means at his disposal to commit the alleged offense, threats made, mental capacity or incapacity, guilt shown by the accused's conduct, his flight, escape, and concealment are some of the circumstantial facts and conduct which often prove important to successful prosecution.

Real Evidence

Real evidence is furnished by objects themselves, on view or inspection, as distinguished from a description of them by a witness. This is evidence that is physical in nature, or, demonstrative. It is directed to the senses without the intervention of witnesses. It is the presenting in court of objects or persons for the observation of the tribunal.

Real evidence is simply evidence which speaks for itself. It requires no explanation, merely identification. Such evidence is extremely important, not only because of its effect on the jury, but because of the range covered. There have been cases in which the aroma of whiskey and the music of an aria were admitted as real evidence. Photographs, moving pictures, X-rays, maps, diagrams, experiments conducted in court, and views of premises are all examples of real evidence.

Scientific crime detection continues to emphasize the importance of such evidence, particularly in regard to the person of the defendant. Fingerprints, photographs, footprints, and handwriting are invaluable tools of enforcement, to mention a few of the many examples here.

Presumptions

The word *presume* occupies an important position in the field of evidentiary law, and has a meaning every private detective should know. A *presumption* is an inference as to the existence of one fact from the existence of some other fact founded upon previous experience of their connection. There are two major types of legal presumptions: conclusive and rebuttable.

Conclusive presumption is considered final, unanswerable, not to be overcome by contradictory evidence, e.g. children under the age of seven are conclusively presumed to be incapable of committing a crime.

Rebuttable presumption may be overcome by proof of its falsity, e.g. presumption of innocence. Various reasons underlie different rebuttable presumptions. Some of them represent short-cuts in proof, some recognize that the opposing party is better able to bring forth proof, and some reflect elements of public policy. Their fundamental function consists of putting the burden on the proper party to establish particular facts.

Hearsay Evidence

Hearsay evidence is based not on a witness's personal knowledge but on matters told him by another. It implies the possession of information by the witness, but not knowledge.

Generally, hearsay evidence is inadmissible. It is admitted only where it appears to be necesssary and trustworthy. It must also fall within the accepted exceptions to the hearsay rule.

The reasons for excluding hearsay are that it violates the rule that all testimony must be given under oath. Also, there is no opportunity to cross-examine the person making the statement. In criminal prosecutions, hearsay violates the rule that a person is entitled to face his accusers. There is as well a great risk of inaccuracy in the repetition of a story. Finally, the general unreliability of such evidence has been determined by experience.

While hearsay evidence is generally inadmissible, the courts recognize that justice will not be done unless certain exceptions to the rule are permitted. In order to provide for such contingencies, the courts have laid down a primary rule of evidence governing hearsay. The following are the principal exceptions to the hearsay rule:

Confessions expressed—A confession is any voluntary acknowledgment in expressed terms against interest made by the defendant in a criminal case. It is a voluntary statement or acknowledgment by an accused person that he or she committed the offense or assisted in its commission.

Criminal admissions—An admission is a voluntary statement or
act made by a party in interest, which is sought to be used against
him at the time of trial. It differs from confession in that a confession is an acknowledgment in expressed terms by a party of his
guilt. An admission is a statement made by the accused and tending, with other evidence, to prove his guilt.

Dying declaration—A dying declaration is made by a person who,
at the time of the statement, knew that he was dying and felt that
death was inescapable.

Res gestae—The term *res gestae* is derived from two Latin words,
res meaning things, and *gestae,* meaning same origin. Thus, things
so intimately connected with the point at issue as to form a part of
it are res gestae, or things of the same origin. Spontaneous declara-
tions preceding or immediately following an act at issue are
admitted in evidence as exceptions to the hearsay rule for the
reason that speaking the truth is regarded as instinctive. If a man
speaks before he has time to think, to make up a story, or fabricate
a lie, he will speak the truth ordinarily.

There are a number of important tests which determine whether
or not an evidentiary fact will be admitted as res gestae:

- The statement or action must precede, be concurrent
  with, or follow the main act very closely in point of
  time.
- It must be of such a spontaneous character as to pre-
  clude the possibility of fabrication.
- The declaration or statement must *not* have been made
  in response to a question.
- It must tend to elucidate and explain the character and
  quality of the act.
- In general, only the person who committed or partici-
  pated in the act or witnessed it may be the declarant.

It is difficult to draw a line and say when a declaration is too
remote from the occurrence to be admissible. It may precede, follow, or be concurrent with the act and can be admitted to describe
the circumstances leading to the act, motive, or intent.

Where the statement accompanies the act, little difficulty is
encountered. When time intervenes, however, particular circumstances must determine whether or not the statement is sufficiently related to the act. The important thing to a private
detective is that the statements made just before, during, or just
after crimes or other startling occurrences, when relevant and

material and made under the stress of nervous strain and excitement involving such happenings, can be admitted in evidence as part of the res gestae.

Public records or reports—Courts have taken the position that a record made by a public official in the course of his duties should be reliable and of sufficiently high repute to be admissible as evidence. They reason that it would tend to disrupt the machinery of government if the recording official had to go into court and testify to the facts described in the record. Moreover, a public record is admitted in its original form because it would often be difficult, if not impossible, to have the recording official testify. Distance, death, and periodic changes in office are a few of the reasons here.

Public records or reports may be admitted as an exception to the hearsay rule under the following circumstances:

- The record must be made in the course of the official duties of a public officer.
- The record must be made with the personal knowledge of the recording official.
- In general, a public record is not admissible if it involves an exercise of judgment or discretion on the part of the recording official.
- A properly authenticated and certified copy of a public record is admissible.

Regular entries in the course of business—The courts reason that an entry made in the conduct of a regular business is sufficiently credible to make it admissible as hearsay evidence. There are four major tests by which the admissibility of a regular entry in the course of business is determined:

- The entry must have been made about the time of the occurrence of the fact at issue.
- The entry must have been made in the usual course of business.
- The entry must have been made with the personal knowledge of the person making the entry, or if the system is too complex to permit that, then the regularity of the bookkeeping system must be shown.
- The original entry in the book must be offered.

Matters of pedigree—Pedigree is usually defined as a record of ancestry; lines of descent; lineage. As employed in evidentiary law, pedigree involves a matter of parentage or relationship, including birth, death, marriage, family relationships.

Formerly, much of our knowledge relating to pedigree was based upon statements by members of the family. Only in relatively recent years has such information become registered in permanent form by legally established governmental agencies. When such data is registered, courts will take judicial notice of them and it is not necessary to resort to the hearsay of members of the family or persons acquainted with the facts. But where the question of pedigree is some years back, usually there is no living witness who has personal knowledge of the circumstances. It therefore becomes necessary, if any proof at all is to be forthcoming, to resort to statements of others who knew of the fact through hearsay.

The broad scope of the rule indicates its importance. The fact of marriage may prove a deciding factor in adultery and bigamy cases and in cases involving divorces, child abandonment, and assault. Age becomes an issue of exceptional importance in crimes involving juveniles. The defendant's capacity to commit a crime may hinge on his age, and the age of the person upon whom the crime is committed may determine the nature of the charge. As in other exceptions to the hearsay rule, courts have laid down certain tests to determine the admissibility of pedigree evidence. Among these are:

- Testimony as to pedigree is usually restricted to members of the family, old friends, and family servants.
- The declaration must have been made before the beginning of the controversy in which the question of pedigree arises.
- The statement will usually be received only when the person who made it is dead.

Reported testimony—It sometimes happens that a second trial becomes necessary in a criminal proceeding. Some of the grounds set forth by statute for holding such a trial are misconduct of the jury, a verdict or decision contrary to the evidence, evidence admitted or rejected contrary to the law, and irregular court proceedings which thereby prevent a fair and impartial trial. In such cases, whether or not testimony given at the first can be used in the second trial may become a matter of importance.

If a witness at the first trial is still alive at the time of the second trial, and can be called upon to testify again, there is no problem. But suppose one of the principal witnesses in the first trial dies or leaves the jurisdiction before the second trial is called? In such cases, reported testimony of one trial is admissible in a second trial as an exception to hearsay. Thus, the testimony of such a witness is not lost.

The reported testimony rule may be stated as follows: testimony given by a witness at a former trial is admissible in any subsequent action or proceeding where it appears that the witness has since died or is beyond jurisdiction permanently or indefinitely, if the parties and questions at issue are substantially the same. Reported testimony is admitted by the courts for several reasons. Reliability of testimony is assumed by the court since the original testimony was given under oath at a preceding trial and was subject to cross-examination.

Hence, there is no violation of the constitutional provisions conferring upon the accused person the right to be confronted by a witness against him.

Testimony given in a preceding trial will not be admitted unless the following tests are met:

- The reported testimony must have been given in a previous trial or preliminary hearing involving the same defendant as in the second trial.
- The second trial must involve the same crime (or another of similar nature) as the first trial or preliminary hearing and must grow out of the same set of facts as the first trial or hearing.
- The witness whose former testimony is offered is dead, out of the jurisdiction of the court, or otherwise completely unavailable.
- The statements made at a former trial or hearing may be reported by any witness who heard them or by stenographic notes taken at the time.

Corpus Delicti

Corpus delicti translated from Latin means body of the offense, or in other words, the facts and situations which go to make up the commission of the crime. Since crimes involve some specific loss or injury, the loss or injury must first be proved, i.e., a house burned in an arson case, property missing in a larceny case, a person dead in a murder case, and so on. Moreover, since someone was involved in the commission of the act, the person or persons responsible must be identified where possible. Thus, corpus delicti, or body of the offense, actually includes all facts relating to the commission of a particular crime and the further fact that the crime was committed by some human agent. There are a number of judicial principles governing corpus delicti which should be kept in mind:

- A confession cannot be used to establish corpus delicti.
- Proof of corpus delicti must be sustained before conviction can follow.
- Corpus delicti need not be proved conclusively, nor even beyond a reasonable doubt. The rule is met if there is sufficient corroborative evidence to show the existence of an offense.
- Proof of corpus delicti may be made by direct, real, or circumstantial evidence, or any combination of these. If evidence meets the usual tests of admissibility, it can be used to substantiate corpus delicti.
- As a rule, the more grave the case, the more strict will be the court's interpretation of the rule.

Best Evidence Rule

The *Best Evidence Rule* provides that one shall present in court the best available evidence of the fact you are seeking to establish. Example: when the private detective goes into court on a motor vehicle accident case, he produces pictures and diagrams of the roadway where the accident occurred. Pictures and diagrams are, therefore, admissible since the detective can't bring the roadway into court.

In all questions of admissibility, the burden of providing the competency of the evidence falls upon the person seeking to introduce it. In other words, if the prosecution wants to introduce a photograph of a gun, the defense lawyer does not have to prove that it is not the best evidence. The defense need only object, and it is up to the prosecution to prove that it is in fact the best evidence available. If no objection to the submission of such evidence is raised, it will be admitted. The judge is merely an umpire. In such a circumstance, he will probably raise no objection himself.

Courtroom Testimony

The private detective will be called upon many times to testify in a court of law. He must present any evidence that he has obtained from his investigation and answer questions from the subject's attorney.

There are several rules that a private detective must keep in mind when giving courtroom testimony. They are:

- Have a neat appearance.
- Know your report inside and out.
- Do not rely on your memory.
- Always tell the truth.
- Be polite, even if ruffled by the subject's attorney.
- Be professional.

Cross-Examination

After the private detective testifies for his client's side, he will be subjected to cross-examination from the opposing attorney. Here, the opposing attorney will try certain tactics in order to trip up your preceding testimony and thus make you appear to the jury as an unreliable witness.

The following are some common tactics of cross-examination used by the opposing attorney:

Rapid-Fire Questions	To confuse the private detective. An attempt to force inconsistent answers.
Detective's Response	Take your time in answering the questions. If you did not hear or understand the question, ask to have it repeated.
Repetitious Questions	To obtain conflicting and/or inconsistent testimony from the private detective.
Detective's Response	Listen carefully and politely. State that you have answered that question already.
Over-Friendly Attorney	To get the private detective to give favorable testimony.
Detective's Response	Be aware of this tactic because the opposing attorney will try to discredit your testimony.
Badgering the Witness	To make the private detective angry so that he will lose his cool and his logic.
Detective's Response	Stay calm and remember this tactic.
Staring	The opposing attorney will pause and stare between the questions in an attempt to make the private detective feel uneasy.
Detective's Response	Do not get ruffled. Wait patiently for the next question.

REVIEW QUESTIONS

1. What is evidence?
2. What are the three principal tests for admissibility of evidence?
3. What is meant by burden of proof?
4. What is direct evidence?
5. What is circumstancial evidence?
6. What is real evidence?
7. What is the difference between conclusive and rebuttable presumptions?
8. Under what circumstances may hearsay evidence be introduced in a court of law?
9. What is corpus delicti?
10. What is the best evidence rule?

4. Criminal Investigation

Throughout his career, the private detective will be involved in criminal investigations. The following chapter covers all aspects of a criminal investigation. The private detective must keep in mind that the police will be first to handle serious criminal cases. This is dictated by law. There will still be work left for the private detective, however.

For example, the private detective is retained to investigate criminal charges lodged against a person. The private detective could be retained by the subject's attorney, wife, or an interested party who believes the subject is innocent of the charges. The private detective in this case will retrace the whole case and try to find evidence that will prove the subject innocent.

Or the private detective will be retained by some business organization in order to investigate some type of theft that has occurred. Many times businesses do not want to involve the police because it might prove embarrassing.

Many of the areas covered in the criminal investigation text will not be part of the private detective's tasks. Again, it is because the police will handle the criminal investigation first. This part of the text will show how information and evidence is obtained by the police and how it can be used by the private detective. It will also enlighten you on how a complete criminal investigation is performed.

Qualities of an Investigation

There are four qualities to an effective investigation. The investigation must be objective, thorough, relevant, and accurate.

Objective

All private detectives must be willing to accept any fact uncovered in the investigation even if it does not agree with his personal opinions.

Thorough

The private detective must check out each lead or bit of information no matter how small it seems. He must also recheck them to make sure they remain consistent.

Relevant

The private detective must use only that information uncovered in the investigation that pertains to the subject of the investigation. Use only that evidence which tends to prove or disprove the matters under investigation.

Accurate

The private detective must produce evidence that is free from mistakes and conforms to the truth. Again, the private detective must double-check all information.

Preliminary Investigation

The first step is for the private detective to establish that the crime under investigation did in fact occur. Next, the private detective proceeds to find out the exact manner in which the crime was carried out. This may reveal a motive. The private detective must not leave any stone unturned because the information that would break the case might be uncovered.

The next step is to locate any physical evidence that might be at the crime scene (see *Physical Evidence*).

The fourth step is to interview the victim as well as locating all witnesses or possible witnesses for subsequent interviewing (see *Interviewing Techniques*).

Follow-up Investigation

At this point, the private detective must interview and obtain statements from all the witnesses. He must canvas the area to locate other witnesses who did not step forward during the preliminary investigation. The private detective must also determine who would have a motive to commit the crime or who would benefit from the crime, as well as obtaining the results from the examination of the physical evidence that was found at the scene.

Once all the information is in, the private detective must analyze it all and start to put the pieces together. Sometimes, witnesses or victims might have to be interviewed again in light of your deductions or new evidence.

Concluding the Investigation

The conclusion to your investigation is put forth in your final typewritten report. The case can be closed by identifying and apprehending the suspect, recovering the stolen property, and preparing an airtight case, or the case is left open because no conclusions can be drawn at this time and the appearance of new evidence could solve the case. If a case is going to be left open, make sure that all leads were followed up and that no logical conclusion can be drawn at this time.

Investigative Questions

A thorough investigation requires that specific questions must be answered which link the crime, the perpetrator, and the victim. The investigation must answer:

WHO questions

- Who discovered the crime?
- Who reported the crime?
- Who saw or heard anything of importance?
- Who had a motive for committing the crime?
- Who committed the crime?
- Who helped the perpetrator?
- With whom did the suspect associate?
- With whom are the witnesses associated?

WHAT questions

- What happened?
- What crime was committed?
- What are the elements of the crime?
- What were the actions of the suspect?
- What do the witnesses know about the case?
- What evidence was obtained?
- What was done with the evidence?
- What tools were employed?
- What weapons were utilized?

- What knowledge, skill, or strength was necessary to commit the crime?
- What means of transportation was used in the commission of the crime?
- What was the motive?
- What was the modus operandi?

WHERE questions

- Where was the crime discovered?
- Where was the crime committed?
- Where were the suspects seen?
- Where were the witnesses during the crime?
- Where was the victim found?
- Where were the tools and weapons obtained?
- Where did the suspect live?
- Where did the victim live?
- Where did the suspect spend his leisure time?
- Where is the suspect now?
- Where is the suspect likely to go?
- Where was the suspect apprehended?

WHEN questions

- When was the crime committed?
- When was the crime discovered?
- When was notification received?
- When did the police arrive at the scene?
- When was the victim last seen?
- When was the suspect apprehended?

HOW questions

- How was the crime committed?
- How did the suspect get to the scene?
- How did the suspect get away?
- How did the suspect get the information necessary to enable him to commit the crime?
- How was the crime discovered?
- How did the suspect secure the tools and weapons?
- How were the tools and weapons utilized?
- How much damage was done?
- How much property was stolen?

- How much skill, knowledge, and strength was necessary to commit the crime?

WHY questions

- Why was the crime committed?
- Why were the particular tools utilized?
- Why was the particular method employed?
- Why were the witnesses reluctant to talk?
- Why was the crime reported?

Search

The search of the crime scene should be systematic. Start at the entrance and check the ground or floor first for marks, stains, etcetera. Eliminate all large objects not connected with the crime. If the crime scene is indoors, examine walls, stairways, windows, and so on. Note all findings without unnecessary touching. Then note pertinent articles of evidence and their relationship to one another and to the scene in general. The scene and all evidence should be preserved in their original positions until photographs have been taken. Then smaller objects can be searched such as desks, shelves, diaries, letters, photographs, etcetera. The search should be extended beyond the immediate scene, noting vegetation, marks on soil, and so on (see *Physical Evidence*).

Observation and Deduction

Detailed observations should be made, noting especially anything unusual. Careful note should also be made of what would be expected to be found at the scene if conditions were normal. So-called "luck" in investigation comes from diligent work. Observation without investigation and deduction is of little or no value.

Reconstructing the Criminal Action at the Scene

At first, the investigator should not imagine himself in the position of the criminal. He should try to deduct the type of criminal from the method of operation used and loot taken. The detective should then try to imagine how that type of criminal would behave. The possibility that the crime may have been committed by more than one person must also be considered.

The route of approach or means of arrival, the action at the scene, and course of departure are the three major sources for most evidence. All evidence and deductions are to be noted. The investigator should tear down and rebuild his preliminary reconstruction until every piece of evidence is fitted into the picture. Circumstances before and leading up to the crime should be considered in the reconstruction. However, until proof is obtained, all reconstruction at the scene is theoretical.

The preliminary reconstruction is of value in questioning and analyzing statements of witnesses and suspects. It gives a starting point to the investigation. The theory must be abandoned as soon as proof shows it is inconsistent with facts uncovered. Every theory should be investigated to an end. Nothing should be taken for granted. When discarding a theory, it should not be entirely eliminated from the mind. The ability to judge when a theory should be abandoned is a valuable asset to the investigator.

Recording the Crime Scene

Notes are a great aid in recording a crime scene, especially during a prolonged investigation. A notebook and pencil should be carried and used by the investigator. Everything observed should be noted if of value or thought to be of value in the investigation. Full and complete notes should be recorded, including full names and addresses, full descriptions of persons, places, and things, and times. Later, the unimportant can always be eliminated.

Notes should be taken at the time of the examination. If open note-taking is resented by persons, mental notes should be taken and put in writing as soon as possible thereafter. Notes should not be biased. They may be used in court. From concise notes, clear understandable reports are made. Notes are to be kept in proper sequence. Everyday notes should be kept in a daily file. With court permission, a witness can refresh his memory by referring to his written notes.

Sketches are often important for the prosecution because they outline the facts and give a clearer perception. Sketches should be neither too complicated nor too meager. Sketches and photographs are closely related in connection with crime. The sketch particularly indicates exact distances and positions of objects. The photograph shows details. Both should be used. Sketches are of value because they preserve descriptions and locations of important evidence before it is moved or destroyed. The sketch can be used when questioning witnesses. Better observations can be made and better statements taken. Witnesses can indicate on the sketch actions taken.

Photography represents an important aid to criminal investigation. A primary purpose of photographs here is to identify and obtain information about criminals and unknown or missing persons. They can also preserve and identify evidence, and aid in prosecuting the criminal.

Photographs give an accurate picture of the original crime scene before anything is moved. They also can help to refresh memory, thus giving a better understanding of the scene. Photos can reveal evidence not noticed at the original scene.

Note that photos are important to the prosecutor because they will acquaint him with the original crime scene and details. He can thus better understand statements made, and can better question witnesses. Photos will help him in the preparation and presentation of his case. They can also help to prove or disprove alibis made by witnesses or the accused.

Photos are important to the court and the jury because they acquaint them with the original scene and all its details. They can better understand testimony, evidence, and exhibits that are presented through the photos.

Reenacting the crime and criminal's movements on film gives a true record of occurrences. When photographing the scene and evidence, a general scene photograph is first taken, then photographs of the route of approach, the spot of commission, and the route of exit. If possible, photographs should be taken under the same conditions as when the crime occurred. Close-ups of wounds on the victim should be taken before and after washing. Photos should show the relationship of wounds to features of the person to identify the wounds with the victim. Notes of all photos taken are made in the notebook, including date, hour, lighting, compass directions, witnesses, and subject. Photographs have a psychological effect in court. All photographs should be examined before court for any misleading factors. Investigators should be familiar with all photographs in the case. If distortions or flaws show, or the scene has been disturbed, the photographer must be prepared to explain. No data should be written on backs of the photographs.

REVIEW QUESTIONS

1. What are the four qualities of an effective investigation?
2. What are the various steps involved in a preliminary investigation?
3. What are the basic questions that must be answered in all investigations?
4. What are the three ways a private detective can record a crime scene? What is the purpose and importance of each?
5. Why is it important for the private detective to reconstruct the criminal action while at the scene of a crime?

5. Physical or Real Evidence

Physical or real evidence are the terms used to describe any and all objects as they pertain to a crime. Such evidence can be sent to a crime laboratory where it can be analyzed. The analysis can aid by answering, or by helping to answer, the questions of whether a crime has been committed, how and when it was committed, who committed it, or who could have committed it. This is accomplished by comparisons of unknown objects and substances to known objects and substances.

Nearly all evidence at the scene or in the investigation has a relationship to the perpetrator, either through possession, use, or association. The investigation of the scene is to be made as soon as possible, before any evidence is moved or destroyed. Evidence is of great value in assisting the investigator to:

- Reconstruct the crime.
- Identify the perpetrator.
- Destroy the alibi of the suspect when apprehended, and assisting the prosecutor by demonstrating definitely the criminal's complicity, without which successful prosecution would be difficult, if not impossible.

Two types of evidence may be found at scenes of crimes:

Immovable or Fixed—Footprints, tire or tool marks, latent fingerprints, markings or writings on objects too bulky to remove, etcetera. Cannot be gathered; preserved by photographing, sketching, lifting, casting, and notes.

Movable—Firearms, documents, liquids, stains, dust, debris, wood, metals, etcetera. Can be gathered and preserved for use by the investigator for presentation in court.

37

Gathering Evidence

The manner in which evidence is gathered and handled will reflect the ability or carelessness of the investigator when the case is presented in court. All evidence should be gathered and secured. That which later proves of no value can be eliminated. The continuity of possession should be unbroken from the crime scene right through to the trial. Receipts should be obtained. As few persons as possible should handle the evidence.

Perishables should be preserved by refrigeration. All liquids must be well-stoppered, and clean glass containers used. Store away about four ounces. Solids are stored in the amount of one pound. Allow nothing to touch, mutilate, disturb, contaminate, or destroy such perishables.

Any material that cannot be definitely identified by the investigator should be gathered and forwarded to the laboratory for identification and complete analysis. It should be delivered as quickly as possible, accompanied by a report with all details regarding the evidence and what tests are requested. The evidence should be sufficient to allow necessary tests to be made, properly marked for identification, and wrapped, preserved, and transported carefully and properly. Any material or evidence forwarded for comparison with the suspect should be wrapped separately and clearly identified as such. The investigator must allow the laboratory sufficient time to make proper and complete tests and examinations.

Stains

A stain can be caused by blood, seminal fluid, body fluid, paint, oil, wax, grease, syrups, dyes, inks, acids, mud, or vegetable matter. Stains can be involved in cases of homicide, suicide, arson, rape, and most other crimes.

Stains caused by mud, paint, rust, food, or vegetable matter may appear to be blood. Deductions should not be made until the stain is analyzed by the laboratory. The collection process must be done in such a manner so as not to contaminate the sample. All movable objects that are stained should be gathered and placed in clean containers. If the stain is wet and is on an immovable object, sterile cloth can be used to blot up the stain. Depending on the immovable object, sections containing the stain can be cut out and submitted to the laboratory. If the stain is dry and is on an immovable object, scrapings of the dried stain can be taken. After submission, the laboratory evaluates the substance in order to answer the following questions:

- What is the substance that caused the stain?
- If it is blood, is it animal or human?
- What type of animal did the blood come from?
- What is the blood type?
- If it is mud, what is the geological source?
- What is the area of origin?
- If vegetable matter, what type of plant?
- Where does it grow?
- If it is a man-made or refined item, like dyes, oil, paints, inks, acids, etcetera, who manufactured it?
- Where was it manufactured? Who distributed the product?

Fingerprints

Fingerprints, either visible or invisible to the naked eye, make up the next type of evidence. Fingerprints may be involved in any crime. Every surface believed to have been touched by the criminal should be searched for prints. A special process must be used in order to raise latent prints, which are invisible to the eye. Chemical dusting powders are used to raise such prints. Once the print is visible, a photograph should be taken. Then a special tape is used to lift the print so that it can be transferred onto a plain white index card. If the visible prints or dusted latent prints are on movable objects, those objects should be carefully wrapped and sent to the laboratory.

Firearms

Firearms and related items such as handguns, rifles, shotguns, machineguns, bullets, shells, cartridges, and powder make up the next type of physical evidence. Firearms and related material can be involved in cases of homicide, suicide, accidental death, robbery, malicious mischief, and assault and battery. The found evidence should be handled and wrapped so as not to destroy any fingerprints, surfaces, heads of shells, or rifling grooves on bullets. The item should be packaged so that no knocking or rubbing occurs. Each piece of evidence should be wrapped separately in clean paper or absorbent cotton. Firearms should be carefully suspended without wrapping or rubbing of any kind. Firearms can be placed in a large plastic bag.

The laboratory, after examining the bullet, may be able to identify the manufacturer and caliber of the bullet. The laboratory, after a comparison of a bullet taken from the victim and a bullet fired from a gun that was found or confiscated, can conclude whether or not the bullet was fired from that particular gun.

Questioned Documents

Questioned documents are another type of evidence, such as letters, statements, checks, ledgers, records, or any other type of written document. Questioned documents can be involved in cases of threat, extortion, forgery, counterfeiting, kidnapping, fraud, embezzlement, malicious mischief, gambling, libel, or obscenity. The evidence must be handled very carefully so as not to destroy fingerprints thereon. Do not fold, crush, rub, crack, mark, or smear the document. Evidence should be placed in a plastic bag and sealed. Samples of writings should be obtained for comparison, and should be done on the same writing surface, using the same implements, printers, typewriters, and if possible, the same words and letters that were used in the questioned document. Handwriting samples should also be gathered from all suspects. Such samples can be gathered from the suspect's home, office, club, bank, gas and electric company, from records at city hall, or the motor vehicle bureau.

After analysis, the laboratory may have answers to the following questions:

- Are the two samples of handwriting from the same person?
- Was the document forged?
- What type of writing instrument was used?
- If a pen was used, who manufactured it?
- If a typewriter was used, who manufactured it?
- Are the two samples of type from the same typewriter?

Inert Substances

Wood, metal, plastic, paper, glass, dust debris, and so on are all inert substances. They can be involved in any type of criminal case.

The evidence must be collected so that it does not become contaminated. Carefully chip, scrape, brush, or gather the evidence and place it into clean containers. After analysis, the laboratory may answer the following questions:

- What is it?
- What type is it?
- Who manufactured it?
- Where did it come from?

Impressions

Reproductions in the third dimension are made chiefly of tire marks, footprints, teeth marks, and tool marks. Plaster of paris is generally used. Many times good reproductions cannot be made because they have been distorted either by man or by weather conditions. Impressions should always be photographed before casting is attempted. Correct measurements should be taken. A sketch should be made, noting in particular the individual marks of identification in the pattern. All reproductions should be marked for identification. In the study of a reproduction of the mark, consideration should be given to the weight of the subject and the construction of the soil, snow, foodstuff, wood, etcetera. Much valuable information regarding objects and persons can be gained from a careful scientific study of marks left by persons or objects.

Reproduction of evidence in plastic form is important. It preserves the object in an objective way. However, it has limitations. Marks are rarely complete, are seldom preserved to remain intact, and will not always reproduce in good fashion. This may be due to lack of knowledge and experience of the caster, or lack of proper working tools and materials. Only through practice and experience can good results be obtained.

Recording the marks without sound interpretation is of no value. Specialists in the objects that made the marks should be consulted: shoes—shoemaker; tires—tire manufacturers and repairmen; teeth—dentist; tools—machinists, and so on. The search for marks at the scene of the crime should be extended along the route of approach, at the spot of commission, and along the route of exit.

Liquids

Liquids can also be used in the commission of a crime. Alcohol, benzine, gasoline, chloroform, paint, lacquer, solvents, ammonia, and acids are some examples of liquids that could be involved in a crime. This type of evidence can be involved in cases of arson, murder, suicide, burglary, homicide, or kidnapping.

The liquid evidence should be collected so as not to contaminate the sample. If at all possible, obtain at least four ounces and place in a clean, well-stoppered and colorless glass bottle. After the laboratory analyzes the evidence that was submitted, it may answer the following questions:

- What is the liquid?
- Could it cause death?
- Was it man-made or natural?
- Who refined or manufactured it?
- Who sells the liquid?

Fibers and Hairs

Fibers and hair, such as feathers, wool, hair, fur, linen, cotton, jute, and asbestos, are usually found at the scene of every crime. They can be found on the body, clothing, or in any given area on any object.

Fibers and hairs should be removed and handled with clean fingers. If tweezers are available, they should be used. It is important that the evidence is not crushed, broken, distorted, or cut. The evidence should then be placed in clean envelopes and forwarded to the laboratory. After the laboratory analyzes the fibers, it may answer the following questions:

- Is the evidence fiber or hair?
- If it is hair, is it animal or human? If it is animal, what type of animal?
- If it is fiber, what type? What type of products is it used in?
- Who manufactures the fiber?
- Did the hair fall out, or was it pulled out?
- Is the hair from a male or female?
- From what part of the body did the hair come from?
- What is the race of the person?

Chemical and Instrument Analysis

Any substance submitted can be analyzed chemically or by modern computerized laboratory equipment. The results can reveal:

- The type of substance
- Its composition
- Its properties
- The normal use of the substance
- The effects of the substance
- Unusual characteristics

REVIEW QUESTIONS

1. What is physical evidence?
2. How can physical evidence assist the private detective in his investigation?
3. What are the two types of evidence found at the scene of a crime? Give examples.
4. What can a laboratory analysis determine from a fiber sample?
5. Why is it important to use extreme care when gathering and handling evidence?

6. Developing Leads

There is a wealth of information that can be obtained by anyone. Most of it is public record. This means that a private detective can obtain information without having any problems. Information is stored on the federal, state, county and on the local levels. The following list tells you where to find information.

County Registrar of Voters—names, addresses, places of birth, occupations, and signatures.

County Criminal Records—information on convicted criminals including court sentencing.

Superior Court Files (County)—information on all civil court cases.

Corporation Files (County)—names, addresses, dates of incorporation, corporate officials.

Marriage Files (State)—full names, addresses, dates of birth of both parties.

Birth Records (State)—names, addresses, places of birth, dates of birth, names of parents.

Death Records (State)—names, addresses, dates, and places of death.

Tax Files (County)—names, addresses of owners of all real property, dates of purchase, tax rates.

Motor Vehicle (State)—names, addresses of licensed drivers, ownership of vehicles. Information is hard to get; best to have a contact.

Public Library

The public library has a reference section which will carry the following books:

City Directories which contain cross-reference information on names of people residing in a community, their addresses, phone numbers, occupations, etcetera.

Business Directories which contain cross-reference material on all corporations, their addresses, subsidiaries, corporate offices, products, and service information.

Civil Directories which list all civil employees.

Important People Directories list names, addresses, and contributions of people in all important fields including law, medicine, business, literature, etcetera.

Legal Directory lists the names, addresses, and phone numbers of all attorneys.

Armed Forces Directory lists all active and retired officers.

Magazine Reference Book lists alphabetically and by year all subjects covered in all magazines printed. Also, newspaper articles are kept on file. You can even go directly to the newspaper offices where they have their own library.

Federal Files

In 1975, the amended Freedom of Informations Act was passed. This act allowed the private citizen to obtain just about any bit of information that the federal government has. Of course, there are exceptions which will be discussed later.

First of all obtain a copy of *The Federal Government Registry* which can be bought from the government or borrowed from the library. This book lists every single federal department and division as well as their addresses.

Examples of the different agencies include the F.B.I., C.I.A., Drug Enforcement Administration, U.S. Office of Personnel Management, Veterans Administration, Justice Department, Department of Transportation, State Department, and Customs Service.

Certain federal information cannot be obtained by the private citizen. But if your request does not fit into the following categories, then you have the right to it:

- Secret classification
- Internal personnel rules
- Information that comes under federal law, like income tax or patents.
- Active criminal investigative files
- Geological data
- Commercial trade secrets

- Inter-agency memos
- Files on individuals which if released would constitute an invasion of privacy.
- Files from divisions in charge of financial institutions.

The private detective must write a letter to the appropriate federal agency requesting the information. The federal agency must respond to you in ten days. If they refuse to give you the information or they do not answer at all, you can write another letter in which you are appealing. The federal agency then has twenty days to act on your appeal. If they still do not answer or if they fail to provide you with the information that you requested, you can sue them in federal court.

If any problems or questions arise, write the Freedom of Information Clearinghouse, P.O. Box 19367, Washington, DC 20036. This is a Ralph Nader group which helps people with their rights under the Freedom of Information Act.

Informers

An informer is a person who gives the private detective information about the incident in question and wishes to remain anonymous. There are two types of informers: the professional and the nonprofessional.

The professional informer works for money and is tied into the criminal world. In most cases he will not testify in court because the person he is snitching on might do him some harm. He just provides the private detective with information (leads) that can be developed into evidence. The professional informer should not be seen in public with the private detective because it might compromise his position in the underworld.

The nonprofessional informer volunteers information or can be induced to give information. He is usually in a position where he is exposed to information that you are not aware of. He could be a doorman, a mailman, or a secretary who happened to be in the area when the incident took place.

Release Form

The private detective has to have access to various records that are not open to the public. Included in this area are doctor records, hospital records, insurance records, and so on. To obtain these records, the private detective must obtain a release form signed by the party involved.

The release form should read as follows:

Date _____

This release form authorizes *(Person to receive information)* or their agents, to examine, inspect, or make copies of all *(Name specific record)* of any kind or nature pertaining to *(Specify injury)*, sustained by *(Victim's name)* on *(Date)*, when *(Victim's name)* was involved in *(Type of incident)* with *(Person who was also in the accident)*.

Signature: _____

Witness:

_____

Background Information

Background information is probably one of the most important tools a private detective can use to complete an investigation. The success or failure of an investigation depends upon how much information can be gathered initially. Every single bit of information is a possible lead that can be followed up on. The next page is a background information form. It can be used for investigating criminal cases, divorce cases, accident cases, insurance cases, negligent cases, missing persons, pre-employment cases, property loss cases, and other civil cases.

The background report form on the following page is one of the most important forms that the private detective will use. Let's see how it can develop leads by discussing each category listed on the form.

The background report form should be completed on your initial client contact. If more space is needed, continue on the back of the form.

Heading

The *heading* found in the form's top right corner is used for the private detective's reference. The date and the case number that you assign to the case aids a private detective when filing away paper work or when submitting a bill to a client for services. Just below this you will find a section which will describe the type of

	DATE: CASE NO.
BACKGROUND	__Injury __Accident __PL __BG __DP __MP __Photo

CLIENT
Name: Address: Phone:

Incident:

SUBJECT
Classification:

Name: Address: Phone:

Occupation/Employer: S.S.No.

DOB___ Race___Sex___Ht.___Wt.___Bld.___Hair___Eyes___Comp.___

Marital Status: Depende^ts:

Dress: Veh.&Lic.:   Co-Sub:

Education: Skills:

Military: Criminal:

Friends/Relatives:

Past Res./Vacations: Interests:

Bank/Credit:

Competency: Reason for Absence:

INSURANCE
Insurance Co.:   Coverage:

Insured/Injuries:

Hosp./Doc.:

Witnesses:

Loss
Property Loss:

Remarks:
1.
2.
3.

case. Again, it is only a reference for the private detective. A more detailed case description is in another section of the form.

Injury—refers to any type of bodily injury case.

Accident—refers to car, boat, airplane, pedestrian, industrial, or any other kind of accident.

PL—refers to property loss. It could be property loss due to theft, robbery, arson, etcetera.

BG—refers to all other areas where further information is needed. Included in this area are criminal investigations, pre-employment checks, civil investigations, etcetera.

MP—refers to missing persons.

DP—refers to divorce proceedings.

Photo—refers to the fact that you received a photograph of the subject in question. Aids in identification.

Client

This section is for the private detective's reference. The full name of client must be completed as well as his address. The phone number is also important because undoubtedly you will be calling the client from time to time. The date and time refer to when the incident took place.

Incident—a detailed description of the type of case. In the heading you checked a basic classification. Here, you expand upon it. For example, you checked "accident" in the heading. In the incident block you will put, "Motor vehicle accident, Rt. 22, Johnson Township, N.J." Or you may have checked "BG" (Background) and your case was a rape investigation. Under incident you would put, "Criminal investigation, alleged rape of Mary Jones, 2233 9th St., Lawn, N.J."

Date/time—refers to when the incident took place.

Subject

This section is about the person the private detective will be investigating. Here is where you can gather many leads.

Classification—refers to what relationship the subject has to the case. A sample entry here might be, "The following party alleges that he was injured by the gross negligence of the client."

Name—be sure to get the full name. This insures proper identification.

Address—be sure to get the address of the subject. You may have to set up surveillance at that location. If the subject has moved, you can canvas surrounding apartments or houses and try to ascertain where the subject has moved to.

Phone—just in case you have to contact the subject to set up an interview.

Occupation/Employer—this is needed for background checks or in case you must set up a surveillance at the subject's place of work.

Social Security Number—needed for identification of the subject.

Physical Description—this is vital because you want to make sure that you are following the right person. It is also needed when you are trying to locate a subject (identification purposes).

Marital Status/Dependents—can determine the possible life style and area the subject may live. Also for identification purposes.

Dress—important for locating persons. The private detective can get an idea of how the subject usually dresses.

Vehicle—for identification purposes when tailing a subject or when on surveillance.

Co-Subject—person whom the subject might be involved with.

Education/Skills—information that develops leads on a possible career a fugitive or a missing person might undertake.

Military—information for pre-employment check and also may develop leads on where a subject may be.

Criminal—information for a pre-employment check or to determine what type of criminal life the subject leads. Usually, he will return to the same type of criminal activity and to his same criminal friends.

Friends/Relatives—a lead on the possible whereabouts of a missing person or a fugitive. Girlfriends are included.

Past Residence/Past Vacations—information that may give way to the whereabouts of the subject.

Bank Credit—a check in this area can reveal if the subject really skipped town (he would always take all of his money, or perhaps he had more money than a man of his income should have).

Competency—the physical and mental status of the subject is important because it may give way to several leads. For instance, if the subject is crippled, he needs special doctors and special equipment. Or if the subject has mental problems, he can be irrational and possibly violent.

Reason For Absence—why is the subject missing? Did he have a fight with members of his family or with his employer?

Insurance

This section is utilized when an insurance carrier is involved. It could be an automobile accident, personal injury case, or a property loss case.

Insurance Company—needed because you will be working with them.

Coverage—important to know the extent of coverage when investigating an insurance claim.

Injured/Injuries—names and addresses of all injured. Also the exact injuries sustained. This is important when exposing fraudulent cases.

Hospital/Doctor—areas where medical information can be obtained.

Witnesses—names and addresses of witnesses who observed the incident. Statements from these people can aid greatly in your investigation.

Loss

The exact type, description, amount, and value of property that was lost are listed under this section.

Remarks

Included here are any other bits of information that will aid the private detective in the investigation. Never consider a bit of information too small; it could break the case.

Social Security Account Numbers

The private detective can gain information from a known social security number. The first three digits of the nine digit number indicate the state that the number was issued in. This is an extremely beneficial tool for the private detective to use when trying to locate a subject. Even if the subject has moved several times during his lifetime, the subject may return to the location where he received his social security account number.

Area	First 3 Digits
Alabama	416 - 424
Alaska	574
Arizona	526 - 527, 600 - 601
Arkansas	429 - 432

Area	First 3 Digits
California	545 - 573, 602 - 626
Colorado	521 - 524
Connecticut	040 - 049
Delaware	221 - 222
Florida	261 - 267, 589 - 595
Georgia	252 - 260
Hawaii	575 - 576
Idaho	518 - 519
Illinois	318 - 361
Indiana	303 - 317
Iowa	478 - 485
Kansas	509 - 515
Kentucky	400 - 407
Louisiana	433 - 439
Maine	004 - 007
Maryland	212 - 220
Massachusetts	010 - 034
Michigan	362 - 386
Minnesota	468 - 477
Mississippi	425 - 428, 587 - 588
Missouri	486 - 500
Montana	516 - 517
Nebraska	505 - 508
Nevada	530
New Hampshire	001 - 003
New Jersey	135 - 158
New Mexico	525, 585
New York	050 - 134
North Carolina	232, 237 - 246
North Dakota	501 - 502
Ohio	268 - 302
Oklahoma	440 - 448
Oregon	540 - 544
Pennsylvania	159 - 211
Rhode Island	035 - 039
South Carolina	247 - 251
South Dakota	503 - 504
Tennessee	408 - 415
Texas	449 - 467
Utah	528 - 529

Area	First 3 Digits
Vermont	008 - 009
Virginia	223 - 231
Washington	531 - 539
West Virginia	232 - 236
Wisconsin	387 - 399
Wyoming	520
District of Columbia	577 - 579
Virgin Islands and Puerto Rico	580 - 582
Guam, Samoa and Philippines	586
Railroad Workers	700 - 729

REVIEW QUESTIONS

1. What public information is available to the private detective? On what level of government can that information be found?
2. What categories of information are not available to the private detective under the Freedom of Information Act?
3. What is an informer? What are the two types of informers? Explain the difference.
4. What is the purpose of the background information report?
5. What information can be obtained from the subject's social security number? How can it be used in an investigation?

7. Interviews and Interrogation

Interview Defined

An interview is an informal session where questions are asked to learn facts. The success of the investigation depends upon effective interviewing of complainants, informants, witnesses, suspects, and other people who may have knowledge of the matter under investigation.

The purpose of the interview is to learn what a person has observed through his five senses (sight, smell, hearing, taste, touch). The person being interviewed is presumed to have certain knowledge that may have bearing on the case in question. If the interviewee does not possess knowledge of an incident, the interview should establish that fact. If relevant information is obtained, a formal signed statement should be taken.

The Interview

The private detective should conduct the interview as soon as possible. People have a tendency to forget or mix up information. Expediency is paramount. The private detective must also keep in mind that before the interview, he must carefully and thoroughly plan his interview and must know all aspects of the case in question. One cannot effectively interview when he does not know all the facts.

At all times, the private detective must maintain absolute control of the interview. The first step is that the private detective must help the interviewee feel at ease. This can be accomplished by showing interest in the interviewee's family, job, house, and so on. Next, the private detective should have a positive attitude and project a friendly and businesslike demeanor so that there is no doubt in the interviewee's mind about who is in control of the interview.

There are two types of interviewing approaches: indirect and direct. The *indirect approach* consists of discussion carried on in a conversational manner which permits the interviewee to talk without having to answer direct questions. Persons are more apt to divulge more information when they are being treated as a friend, and do not have to be subjected to a barrage of questions. The *direct approach* consists of direct questioning. This approach is usually employed when the interviewee fears or dislikes your authority, is protecting a relative or a friend, fears reprisals from the criminal, or is unwilling to cooperate because of involvement in the incident.

Interrogation Defined

Interrogation is a formal and systematic questioning to learn facts and obtain admissions or confessions of wrongful acts from persons. The purpose of interrogating a suspect is to obtain an admission or confession of his unlawful act, to obtain a signed statement, and to establish the facts of the crime. This will enable the private detective to obtain direct, physical, or other evidence to prove or disprove the truth of the admission or confession.

The Interrogation

The interrogation should take place immediately if the suspect is apprehended in the act of committing a crime. In all other instances, the interrogation should be conducted only after the facts surrounding the incident have been verified. The interrogation should be conducted in a private place because a person under interrogation is inclined not to reveal confidences in a public place.

The private detective should vary his approach so that it fits the background and character of the person being interrogated, the known facts of the crime, and the real evidence available. The following types of approaches or any combination of them can be used by the private detective:

Direct approach—The private detective assumes an air of confidence concerning the guilt of the suspect by introducing the evidence that is indicative to guilt. The evidence could be either real or consist of testimony from witnesses. The subject should be asked questions that directly relate him to the crime.

Indirect approach—The private detective requests the subject being interrogated to tell all he knows about the crime. Since the private detective has the facts concerning the case, he requires the subject to explain any discrepancies and then endeavors to lead the subject into admissions of truth.

Emotional approach—The private detective tries to arouse and play upon the emotions of the subject. The private detective will point out signs of nervous tension (perspiring, trembling hands, squirming, etcetera) and ask the subject why he is exhibiting such signs. The private detective may point out the moral seriousness of the crime. He may also appeal to the suspect's ego or pride, fears, likes or dislikes, or hate/desire for revenge.

Note Taking

Complete notes are essential to effective investigation and reporting. A majority of the interviewees have no objection to note taking in their presence. Occasionally, some people become reluctant to divulge information when a person is writing down everything that is said. If this occurs, the private detective should not take written notes. Instead, the private detective should just make mental notes. At the earliest time after the interrogation interview, the private detective must then write down the facts.

Statements

The private detective will be called upon to interview a suspect or a witness. The results from your questioning might prove to be of good use to your investigation. At this point in time, the private detective should take a formal signed statement from the subject. Most of the time the private detective will tape-record the statement, have it transcribed to typewritten form, then bring it back to the subject for signing and witnessing. The following is the format that should be used when taking statements.

The first page should contain the following:

STATEMENT

Statement of: (Name, age, and address of person)

Taken at: (Description and address of place where taken)

Time and Date: (Time and date of the statement)

Questions Asked by: (Name and title of questioner)

Notes Taken by: (Name and title of person transcribing tape recorder is applicable)

Witnesses Present: (Names and titles; addresses)

Transcribed by: (Person who did the typing)

The next section of the statement should consist of the following questions and answers.

Q. Mr. (Full Name), my name is _____ of _____ Agency and I would like to ask you some questions regarding circumstances surrounding the (state matter under investigation without revealing any information of damaging importance). Do you, Mr. (full name), voluntarily desire to make a statement regarding this matter or your own free will and accord without any threats having been made to you, and without fear, intimidation, or promise of reward.

A. (Answer)

Q. Mr. _____, this is (all persons who are present are introduced by name and title, and office represented), who are present to hear the statement you are about to make.

Q. What is your full name?
A. _____ .

Q. What is your Date of Birth?
A. _____ .

Q. Where do you live?
A. _____ .

Q. Are you married? (If so, the next questions should be, "What is your wife's name?")
A. _____ .

Q. How many children do you have?
A. _____ .

The above questions and others pertaining to family and personal life are asked to strongly identify the person questioned with the statement taken.

After the personal questions, the subject should be allowed to tell his story, in his own words, without interruption. The investigator takes notes. If his story or statement becomes aimless, the questioner should check him. After he has completed his story, he should then be questioned. Care must be taken in forming the questions to prevent any leading or suggestive questions being asked. Questions should be so worded that they cannot be answered "yes" or "no." Try to get the person to talk as much as possible.

Remember these guiding factors:
1. WHAT happened?
2. WHO did it?
3. HOW did it happen?
4. WHEN did it happen?
5. WHERE did it happen?
6. WHY did it happen?

At the end of the statement, the questions should be as follows:

Q. Did all this happen in (name of county and state)? (Establish venue - locations).
A. _____.

Q. Do you have anything further to tell me?
A. _____.

Q. Please read this statement and if there are any corrections you desire to be made, please state the corrections and I will make them. (If the person is able to write, have him make the corrections in his own handwriting. Statement to be read to person if he cannot read. Use interpreter if the person can't read English. Corrections are made as per request of person questioned. If the statement was tape recorded, play the tape back.)
A. _____.

Q. This statement has been corrected in accordance with your request. Now, is this statement true and correct to the best of your knowledge and belief?
A. _____.

Q. Will you now sign this statement? (If recorded, ask, "Will you sign the statement after it has been tran-

scribed into typewritten form?" Inform party that he
will be permitted to compare the two.)

A. _____ .

The final section of the statement should consist of the
following:

(Signature of person questioned)
(Time and date statement completed)

Witnessed by:

_____ .

_____ .

Note that EACH SHEET of the statement should be signed by the
person making the statement.

Report Writing

The fact that you are the best private detective in the world is
one thing, but if you cannot express yourself on paper, you become
a second-rate private detective. Most of the private detective's contact with the client is through the use of reports. The report submitted must be clear, factual, and accurate. If a person unfamiliar
with the case can pick up the private detective's report and completely understand the case, then you have written a good report.

Purpose of the Report

The purpose of the report is to document in writing a clear
understanding of the facts concerning the investigation. The report
must be clear, concise, complete, and accurate.

A clear and concise formal report begins with the choice of
words and phrases. All statements should be positive; avoid hesi-
tating. This does not mean that you are required to make all short
sentences, or that you should avoid all detail and merely outline
your report, but that *every word* you use adds something definite to
your description.

The report must be complete and include all available information and all of the developments up to the time of its preparation.
To be complete, the report must include both favorable and un-
favorable information. It leaves nothing to chance or misinterpre-
tation and records all data having any bearing on the incident.

The report must also be accurate. This means that all facts must be verified. Names, times, dates, and locations must be precise. Descriptions of persons and incidents should be double-checked. Exact quotes should be used whenever possible, and opinions and hearsay evidence should be avoided except when it is included for a specific reason.

The report should contain the following:

- Absolute facts.
- Answers to the basic interrogatives: who, what, where, when, why, and how.
- Facts reported in a logical sequence.

Types of Report

The private detective will be preparing three general types of reports: preliminary report, follow-up report, and formal report. The *preliminary report* is written documentation of all facts that were gathered during the initial client contact. At this point, the private detective receives background information with which he can start the investigation. All initial leads that have been investigated are reported in this report. They include reporting on what physical evidence was found, and results of interviews with the victim and witnesses.

After analyzing the facts obtained in the preliminary investigation, the private detective can develop more leads which can be followed up on. Reporting on statements taken, new witnesses located, motive established, results of physical evidence testing, deductions, and new evidence should be included in the follow-up report. The *follow-up report* is simply a report on the facts of the investigation that have been developed since the preliminary report was made.

Formal Report

The *formal report* is a final detailed account of the investigation. It is prepared and submitted when all investigative leads have been exhausted and the case has been successfully completed, or in the opinion of the private detective, no conclusions can be made because of the lack of evidence and leads.

Your formal report should be in narrative form, and should be clear, concise, and grammatically correct. Neatness, proper spelling, and proper punctuation are all prerequisites of a good formal report. The formal report should be typewritten and contain the following:

    1. Title Page
    2. Introduction
    3. Body of the Report
    4. Conclusion

The title page should present all information pertinent to the contents of the report. Example:

XYZ Detective Agency
211 Rt. 99
Foxville, NJ 09787

June 9, 1981

Client:	John Jones, Attorney at Law 320 Second Street Rockville, NJ 09088
Case:	Investigation into the activities of one Peter Rapin of 62 59th Street, Youngsville, NJ - Divorce Proceedings
Investigated by:	Detective Peter Lynes

The introduction is the next page of your report, and it should contain a narrative outline of what is contained in the body of the report. It is a brief summary of the findings of your investigation.

The body of the report should present all of your findings that resulted from the investigation. It should be in chronological order. The details should tell clearly what the private detective did, what he learned, who was interviewed, what was said and so on.

Remember, your report should answer the six questions found on page 59. If your investigative report does not answer these questions, then it is incomplete and therefore substandard.

The conclusion is the formal end of your report. Here the private detective makes his concluding statements from the facts gathered in the investigation and/or makes any recommendations that he sees fit.

Importance of Notes

Complete notes are essential to effective investigation and provide the basis for your formal report. If your notes are good, then most likely your report will be good. Your notes should recount every single activity in the course of your day's work. Dates and times must be included. Besides being used for your formal report, notes can help the private detective to recall seemingly unimportant information which may assume more importance as the case is developed.

REVIEW QUESTIONS

1. What is an interview?
2. What is the purpose of an interview?
3. What is the difference between the direct approach and the indirect approach of interviewing?
4. What is interrogation?
5. What is the purpose of note taking during an interview or interrogation?
6. What is the purpose of writing a report? What should the report contain?
7. What is the difference between a preliminary report, a follow-up report, and the formal report?

8. *Surveillance*

Surveillance is the secret observation of persons, places, or things as an investigative technique. Its purpose is to obtain information difficult or impossible to secure in any other manner. There are two types of surveillance: moving and stationary. *Moving surveillance* (or *tailing*) occurs when a private detective follows the subject on foot or by vehicle. *Fixed surveillance* is when the private detective takes a stationary position and observes the subject.

Objectives

The art of surveillance is one of the most important tools that can be used in an investigation. It is quite likely that no other facet of detective work is more amenable to improvement through practice than this one. Surveillance is not, nor should it be, regarded as a haphazard operation. Prior preparation and planning are essential since once the operation has commenced, opportunities to reorganize it are fairly impossible. The objectives of surveillance could be any of the following:

- To obtain evidence.
- To obtain information concerning the nature and scope of the activities of a person.
- To locate a subject by observing his haunts and associates.
- To verify information that was developed during the investigation.
- To obtain information about activities in and around a particular place and to identify all entrants.

65

Preparation

Prior to tailing, the surveillance team should be thoroughly briefed. The nature and background of the subject should be evaluated. The object of surveillance should be well established, and the possible contingencies which might arise should be thoroughly examined. The surveillance team should be familiar with the probable area of operations, and the transportation facilities serving these locations. Also, a knowledge of public buildings, types of occupancy, and character of the population is of the utmost importance. Finally, the surveillance team should avail themselves beforehand of any equipment that they may likely be needing, such as two-way radios, signalling equipment, and vehicles.

Moving Surveillance

There are three classes of moving surveillance or tailing: close, loose, and progressive. *Close tailing* is the following of a person with or without his knowledge. The private detective's main object is to force the hand of the subject to try and make him panic and possibly reveal something. It is a form of psychological pressure. *Loose tailing* is the cautious following of a person so as not to be discovered. The tail should be suspended when it is reasonably assumed that the subject knows he is being followed. Finally, *progressive tailing* is the following of a person, without his knowledge, in stages. For example, the first day, the tailer follows the subject from his home to the bus stop. The second day, a different tailer follows the subject from the bus stop to the subject's destination. The third day, another tailer follows the subject from his destination to wherever the subject goes next.

A moving surveillance operation should have a minimum of two men on the tailing team. A one-man tail is relatively ineffective. The main tailer should maintain contact with the rest of the tailing team. If a subject makes a stop, the main tailer should communicate with the tailing team about the subject's location. When the subject is lost, the tailer should immediately notify the tailing team. It is often possible to second-guess the subject and reestablish contact. If the tailing team prepared fo the surveillance properly, and knows the subject's home and business addresses, hobbies, habits of entertainment, associates, etcetera, then contact may be reestablished.

A good general procedure to follow while tailing is to shorten the distance between the subject and you when the subject is in a crowded area or approaches a bus, train, or other means of transportation. When in sparsely occupied areas, the tailer should lengthen the distance between the subject and himself.

Foot Surveillance

The most effective method for tailing a subject on foot is the *XYZ Method*. The surveillance team is made up of three people who for discussion purposes will be called X, Y, and Z. Tailer X follows the subject, Tailer Y follows Tailer X, and Tailer Z keeps abreast of the subject across the street. If the subject detects one of the tailers, a quick switch can then be made.

If one of the tailers is recognized, that tailer should stay calm and perform some natural act to counter any suspicions the subject may have. Stop to light a cigarette or buy a newspaper, or start a conversation with a passerby. The tailing team should never do anything that might attract the attention of the subject. Act as naturally as you can and avoid running, dodging, hiding, or any similar behavior.

If the subject gets into a subway train or a bus, at least two of the tailers should get on also. The third man should avoid getting on and await notification from the other team members on the subject's location (by two-way radio or other prearranged type of communication.) While on the subway or bus, one tailer should sit in front of the subject, and the second should sit to the rear of the subject. Do not rise when the subject rises. This could be a trick to see if he is being tailed. The tailing team should wait until the subway or bus stops before rising. If it is at all possible, the tailing team should remain seated until the subject leaves the subway car or bus.

The subject might have occasion to enter an elevator. At least one member of the tailing team should enter the elevator and stand behind the subject. The tailer should exit with the subject. Should the subject observe you getting off with him, enter the nearest office. The tail can be picked up as he exits the building. If the subject enters an office and did not observe you, note the room number and name of the firm.

On occasion, a subject may enter a store or restaurant. The tailing team should keep their distance and act as natural as possible.

Automobile Surveillance

Automobile surveillance is not as easy as it may appear. The tailers have to contend with many irregularities that could interrupt the surveillance. Unscheduled and frequent stops caused by traffic jams, traffic accidents, or traffic signals are just a few examples of these irregularities.

The best method is the same one that was just described: the XYZ Method. In this method, Tailer X follows the subject and keeps within one block of him. Tailer Y follows Tailer X and keeps out of the subject's sight. Good two-way radio communication between all three tailers is important so that each tailer knows the direction the subject is travelling and his location. Tailer Z should travel parallel to the subject and be ready to pick up the tail. Positions of the tailers can be changed at any time. This is a good procedure to follow, especially when you think that the subject might be aware that a car is following him. For example, if Tailer X suspects that the subject might be aware of the tail, Tailer X can communicate this to the other team members and change positions. Tailer X can pass the subject and make a turn that would take him away from the subject's route of travel. Tailer Y can move up and take Tailer X's position. Tailer X can work his way back and take up Tailer Y's former position.

Another method of automobile surveillance is called the *Leap Frog Method.* Only two vehicles are used in this type of tail. The first tailer follows the subject and the second stays three blocks behind the first. When the command is given, via the two-way radio, the first tailer passes the subject's car and turns off while the second tailer takes the first tailer's place. The first tailer then makes his way back and assumes the second tailer's position.

Fixed Surveillance

Fixed surveillance is the observation of persons, places, or things from a fixed base. The fixed base could be an apartment, house, store, or room. Observation should be conducted so as not to be noticeable from the outside. In most cases, binoculars or telescopes will be needed to view the subject matter. The setting up, or dismantling of the surveillance must be done in secrecy so that the surveillance activities will not be revealed to the subjects or neighbors.

Notes

Detailed and accurate notes should be kept throughout the surveillance. All observations should be recorded, no matter how insignificant they may seem. The notes will serve as the foundation for your formal report, as well as for briefing each tailing team on the subject's habits, contacts, and locations.

Undercover Operations

Sometimes a private detective is called upon to act as an undercover operative. An undercover operation requires the placement of a private detective in a role or situation where the private detective's real identity is dropped. He assumes an identity in keeping with the case, for the purpose of detecting violations of law, gather evidence for the prosecution of the criminals involved, and to recover items of thefts. Undercover operations are used in those cases where several individuals have been involved in an illegal activity over a period of time. Blackmarketing, counterfeiting, narcotics, fraud, and conspiracy are all good examples of cases that can be investigated using undercover operations.

The main objectives of an undercover operation are:

- To obtain enough evidence to close the case.
- To identify all persons involved in the case.
- To ascertain the methods of the crime of incident, and to recover stolen items.

Preparing for the undercover operation is of the highest importance. The private detective going undercover should fit into the assignment. Above all, he should be resourceful and have initiative, energy, courage, and good judgment.

Remember that the investigator must have any necessary skills that will be required of him while serving in the undercover role. The same holds true with his education and socio-economic background. Similar consideration must be given to the operative's ethnic suitability, and religious background.

After the type of character to be used in the operation is determined, a fictitious background for the undercover operative is prepared. The background should include name, address, schools attended, place of employment, friends, and so on. Arrangements should be made so that if anyone makes inquiries into the background of the undercover operative, the information then received will corroborate the information that is already known.

The undercover detective's personal possessions should also fit his character. This includes clothes, rings, money, vehicle, etcetera. Also included here are the personal tools used in the detective's undercover role.

It is important that the private detective must never carry any articles or credentials that might suggest his true identity. Lastly, the undercover detective should have his role and all related facts memorized. A check should be made before sending the detective out in the field.

While working undercover, the detective should follow these simple rules:

- Avoid intoxicants lest the detective jeopardize the case or allow his true identity to become known.
- The undercover detective should not take notes while performing his role. He should memorize them while working and record them at a later time. If something has to be noted while on the job, be sure that you are alone when making notes.
- While in the undercover role, the detective should avoid bragging or claiming self-importance. This could make the suspect become suspicious.
- Avoid excessive spending. Spending should be in keeping with the role portrayed.
- The undercover detective must never reveal his identity. If arrested he must communicate with his superiors by prearranged means.

Remember: The undercover detective must not incite or create the commission of a crime with the intent to prosecute the subjects involved. This is called *entrapment* and also provides the accused with a convenient courtroom defense.

REVIEW QUESTIONS

1. What is the definition of surveillance?
2. What are the objectives of surveillance?
3. What are the three classes of moving surveillance?
4. Why is it a good practice to have at least two people on a surveillance team?
5. What is a fixed surveillance?
6. What is an undercover operation? What are the main objectives of such an operation?
7. What rules should an undercover operative follow while working undercover?

9. *Homicide Investigation*

The private detective will not be involved in the initial homicide investigation because the law states that this is the responsibility of the police. The private detective will be retained by a client who has an interest in the case.

Homicide Defined

Homicide is a general word referring to all forms of the killing of a human being by another. The word "another," while it usually refers to a human being, does include a corporation in the case of manslaughter. Because all killings do not bear criminal responsibility, homicide may be divided into "non-culpable homicide," which criminal law does not punish, and "culpable or felonious homicide," which is punishable by law.

In order for a private detective to effectively investigate a homicide, he must fully understand the law concerning homicide. The law of homicide varies from state to state. In one state there may only exist one degree of murder while in another there exist two degrees of murder. The principles presented in this text are generally applicable to most jurisdictions.

Nonculpable Homicides

Nonculpable homicide, which because of the circumstances under which it is committed the law does not punish, is divided into two types: justifiable and excusable. In the case of justifiable homicide, as where a executioner executes a criminal by decree of the court, no blame whatsoever is attached and the killing is called justifiable. In the case of excusable homicide, the accused is considered to some degree at fault, perhaps civilly, but the circumstances are not such that criminal punishment is warranted. For example, this holds true where one is negligently, though accidentally, killed by another. The distinction between the two has lost its former significance because today neither is punished criminally.

Generally, the law excuses or justifies homicide when it is committed:

1. By misadventure.
2. In self-defense.
3. In defense of others.
4. To prevent the commission of certain crimes (arson, burglary, murder, rape, robbery, or sodomy).

Misadventure—a killing by misadventure, accident, or misfortune refers to an accidental killing and when such is the case, the law excuses it.

Self-defense—the rule is that a person may protect himself even to the extent of taking another's life where it reasonably appears to be necessary to preserve his own life or to protect himself from serious bodily harm. A private detective, when resisted in lawfully making an arrest, is not justified in killing the offender for the purpose of guarding his person from bodily harm, unless the injury threatened is a serious one. Mere words or threats of personal violence, however abusive, standing alone will not justify a homicide, the reason being that they do not endanger life or render serious bodily harm. Nor can one stand his ground and kill his assistant if he can avoid impending danger from assault by retreating. If he can retreat with safety, he should do so.

Defense of others—the law generally lists the various persons in defense of whom one may go so far as to kill an assailant: wife/husband, child, parent, brother, and sister. The rules pertaining to when, under what conditions, and to what extent one may go in defending those others are generally the same as in the case of self-defense.

To prevent the commission of certain crimes—a killing is excused or justified if the person killed is attempting to commit arson, burglary, murder, rape, robbery, or sodomy. These crimes were felonies under common law, and because of their serious nature, a killing done to prevent the commission of one of them was justified by law.

Culpable or Felonious Homicide

Murder is the willful, deliberate, and premeditated killing of a human being. Willful is used in this connection refers to intent.

More particularly, it means the specific intent to kill. Deliberate refers to the weighing of such intent before carrying it into effect; i.e., thinking the matter over in one's mind. Premeditation means that the commission of the act must have been contemplated; that is, that the mind entertained the design to kill.

A homicide committed in perpetrating or attempting to perpetrate arson, burglary, rape, robbery, or sodomy is considered murder. It need not be willful, deliberate, and premeditated. It is sufficient if the perpetration or the attempt to perpetrate a felony, named above, is shown, and that there was a killing. Thus there need not be specific intent. The commission or attempted commission of the felony supplies the intent. The intent to commit the felony is carried over and added to the act (the killing) and together they constitute murder.

Culpable or felonious homicide constitutes murder when the killing of a human being is done with malice aforethought. The distinguishing characteristic of murder is malice. We can eliminate the "aforethought" as surplusage since it merely means that there was malice at the time the act was committed. If malice is present, the homicide is murder. If no malice is present, the homicide is either manslaughter or else it is justifiable or excusable. Malice in its legal sense means nothing more than an evil state of mind. This malice or evil state of mind is necessary to constitute murder.

In general, the law recognizes the frailty of human nature and places a killing done in the sudden heat of passion or recklessly on a different footing from a killing that is coolly deliberated and determined. Therefore, we have the crime of manslaughter which is a separate and distinct crime from murder.

Manslaughter is an unlawful homicide without malice. A homicide which is not murder and not excusable or justifiable is generally manslaughter. The characteristic that generally distinguishes murder from manslaughter is malice. If malice is present, a homicide, which is neither excusable or justifiable, is murder; if malice is not present then the homicide is manslaughter. Thus, the absence of malice is the essential characteristic of manslaughter.

Causing death by automobile is also criminal homicide. Depending on the jurisdiction, it could be classified as death by auto, manslaughter, or criminally negligent homicide. Basically, a person who shall cause the death of another by driving any vehicle carelessly and heedlessly and with the willful or wanton disregard of the rights or safety of others can be charged with this crime. Mere carelessness or negligence is not enough. Gross or criminal negligence must be present and must amount to a willful intent to do injury, or a wanton and reckless disregard of the rights and safety of others.

Investigative Steps

All principals of developing an investigation apply to homicide investigations. (See *Criminal Investigations*). The private detective should:

- Obtain all personal information on the deceased; full name, age, date of birth, address, habits, etcetera. Record same and verify all information.
- Ascertain who discovered the body and what other persons were present at the crime scene. Record same.
- Ascertain the time and date of discovery.
- Locate and question all witnesses.
- Ascertain if the victim was alive when first discovered. Also, ascertain if the victim made any statements.
- Describe the exact location, position, and appearance of the body.
- Obtain photographs of the body and then of the entire crime scene.
- Obtain the medical examiner's report, which will have a medical opinion on the cause of death.
- Ascertain if the victim's clothing was analyzed, and the findings of said analysis.
- Ascertain the results of the police search of the crime scene. Was any physical evidence found?
- If possible, conduct your own search of the crime scene. Also, check the victim's personal effects for diaries, letters, addresses, telephone numbers, or other documents which may reveal information about the crime.
- Obtain the names and addresses of the victim's associates. Follow up and interview same.
- Ascertain if there was any evidence found outside of the crime scene which could identify the murderer (footprints), identify means of escape (tire impressions or pieces of the car), or identify the direction of escape.
- Ascertain the movements of the victim and/or suspect prior to the crime.

- Ascertain who usually visited the victim at home and at work.
- Ascertain if the victim was involved in some criminal activity. This can be accomplished by making a thorough search of the victim's home and car.
- Check out all statements made by the witnesses.
- Interview all of the victim's friends.
- Analyze all information that is gathered.

Elements of Proof

The solution of the crime of culpable homicide must be proven beyond a reasonable doubt by competent and relevant evidence. The evidence must show that the victim is dead, that the death resulted from an act or omission of the accused, and that the accused had acted in a willful, deliberate, and premeditated manner or was engaged in the perpetration or attempted perpetration of a felony.

REVIEW QUESTIONS

1. What is homicide?
2. When is a homicide considered murder?
3. What is the difference between culpable and nonculpable homicide?
4. If a person, while perpetrating a felony, kills another by accident, why is the person charged with murder?
5. In order to establish proof of culpable homicide, what must the competent and relevant evidence show?

10. Arson Investigation

Arson is becoming one of the most common types of crime being committed. It is essential and important that the private detective know the causes of arson, as well as the specific investigative techiques needed to solve such crimes.

Originally, at the time of common law, arson was an offense against someone's habitation, or the willful and malicious burning of someone's house. Malice was the essence of the crime, but the offense has been materially extended by statute in different states. Through laws enacted, these states changed the definition of arson so that instead of being a crime against habitations, it is now a crime against property. The property can be a building, a house, a car, a boat, or an airplane, among others.

Motive

Arsonists can be classified under three headings: arsonists for profit, arsonists for revenge, and arsonists for "kicks". The category of arsonists for profit is the largest single group. These persons will burn another person's property for hire, or will burn their own property with the desire to defraud the insurer. These fires are started to destroy or damage property in order to collect insurance, as a means of preventing financial loss, or for any other reason that will bring financial gain. The arsonist may be the proprietor or the operator of a business. He may be a person totally unrelated to the fire victim. The arsonist may also be an investor in an unprofitable business who is not directly involved in the business operation. Most of the private detective's work will center around this type of arson.

There are many reasons for committing the crime of arson. The reasons all boil down to the fact that a financial gain is imminent. One common fraudulent practice is to insure merchandise actually in existence at the time the insurance policy is obtained. After the insurance is secured, the store inventory is reduced, either by conducting a bogus sale, or by removing the merchandise to another location. The premises are then set on fire. Following the fire, a claim is submitted to cover the cost of the stock that was allegedly lost. Another type of arson is used by a businessman who finds it necessary to remodel his place of business so that he can meet competition. To accomplish this in the cheapest possible manner, he sets his place of business on fire and collects the insurance. Another example is when an owner of an automobile sets his vehicle on fire. He may be faced with expensive repair bills, and rather than pay for the repairs, he sets his vehicle on fire and collects the insurance.

The person who burns for revenge is "getting even". There may be a number of reasons for a person's wanting to burn the property of another. Some are petty or imagined grievances, while others have greater significance. Jealousy, a disgruntled employee, a competitor, a jilted suitor, a tenant-landlord dispute, and a teacher-student dispute are all characteristic of the revenge arson case.

Following are some typical examples of revenge fires. The burning of churches and other religious buildings will often come under the title of revenge fire. When there are religious or social problems in an area, there will often be an increase in church fires. Often the person setting this type of fire is a fanatical person. In the business world, a store owner finds he has new competition in the area. This new store has a more modern building and better services. He finds he is losing business. To remedy his problem, he reverts to the use of arson against his business competitor. Another common practice of arson for revenge is when a woman burns up her husband's car because she thought her husband was seeing other women.

The pyromaniac fits in the category of an arsonist who sets fires for "kicks". He suffers from a mental illness called *pyromania*. As the illness progresses, the pyromaniac becomes especially dangerous because he has no regard for human life. He possesses a pathological attraction to fires and is happiest when witnessing a fire and its destructive effects. Generally, the pyromaniac has no rational motive for his crimes. He starts fires on impulse. His first attempts are directed against small structures. It is only a matter of time

before he directs his attacks against dwellings, apartment buildings, lumber yards, and forests. Having started a fire, he remains
at the scene to make sure the fire is well ignited and generally
mingles with the bystanders to contemplate his crime. The pyromaniac should be subject to psychiatric rather than penal care.

The prankster also fits in the category of arsonists who set fires
for "kicks". He sets fires merely for the momentary excitement or as
a general retaliation against society. This person, generally youth-
ful and delinquent in more ways than one, has no special attraction
to fires as such, and will be involved in other crimes as well. He is
also a dangerous person, not specifically as an arsonist, but rather
as an uncontrolled and irresponsible troublemaker. His apprehension is therefore much more difficult because his behavior is
erratic, unpredictable, and follows no distinct pattern. He is also a
pathological case, but one with less definite distinguishing characteristics which could simplify his treatment by psychiatric or other
means.

Origin of the Fire

There are three causes of fires:
- Natural causes without human aid.
- Accidents where human action is involved.
- Incendiary.

It is a rule of law in regard to an arson case that every fire is
initially presumed to be of accidental origin. This presumption
must be overcome before a case can be made. Therefore, it must be
proven that the building was burned by criminal design.

Proof

In order to constitute the crime of arson, there must be a willful
and malicious intent to start a fire or cause an explosion which
results in the loss, damage, or destruction of property. If a person
sets a fire or causes an explosion to property while engaged in the
commission of some crime, it is considered arson. This act, committed with the intention of perpetrating a crime, whether it be a
felony or misdemeanor, is arson because the very recklessness of
the act supplies the willful intention.

If a suspect is directly accused of arson, it is necessary to show by
facts or circumstances, or both, that he could and actually did set
the fire or cause the explosion. If the accused procured another to
commit arson, or if they aided or abetted in the crime, they are both

equally guilty and liable to prosecution. Once the crime of arson is established, every fact or circumstance tending to place any light on the case is usually admissible as evidence against the accused.

Investigatory Procedures

The first step of the investigative process is for the private detective to ascertain if a deliberate fire was set. Expert opinions from the fire department should be sought. Most large fire departments have men specially trained in arson investigation. The private detective should then search the burned building for various signs of arson which could be used in court. The search should start at the approximate location where the fire began. Information gathered from the fire department will help establish the location.

The private detective should search for any of the following pieces of physical evidence that could be used for an incendiary fire:

- Inflammable liquids, such as gasoline, kerosene, alcohol, turpentine, ether, benzine, and naptha.
- Empty containers which could have contained inflammable liquids. Residues of the substance will still be in the empty container.
- Alarm clocks which could be used to set off a detonating device.
- Gunpowder trails or gunpowder residue.
- Paper trails.
- Electric heaters near inflammable materials.
- Candles that could have started the intentional fires.
- Phosphorus or residue of phosphorus
- Pieces of string and matches.
- Rope and matches.
- Cigarette and matches.

In many cases of arson, the perpetrator plants more than one device in the building. This insures that at least one of them will go off. Because the devices are usually separated from one another, there is a chance, especially if the building is not completely destroyed, that one of the devices is still intact.

All procedures covered earlier in the *Criminal Investigation* and *Physical Evidence* chapters should be applied to arson investigation.

Investigative Inquiry

Interviewing victims, witnesses, and neighbors, and then following up on that information, is a very important part of the arson investigation. The same techniques as outlined in the *Interviewing* section should be applied.

Specific questions that should be directed to the victims are:

- What is your full name and address?
- Do you have any enemies?
- Did you have any recent visitors?
- Was there any unusual activity around the premises just prior to the fire?
- Who else has keys to the property?
- Have you ever experienced a previous fire?
- Where did you live before moving to your present address?

Specific questions that should be directed to witnesses and neighbors are:

- What is your full name and address?
- Where were you at the time of the fire?
- Where did the fire originate?
- Who discovered the fire?
- Who turned in the fire alarm?
- What was the nature of the fire when you first discovered it?
- Was there any indication of an explosion?
- Did you see any persons and/or vehicles around the premises?
- Did you notice any recent visitors to the premises?
- Did you notice anything being removed from the premises?
- Do you recall any other fires that had taken place at the premises?

The private detective must also look into the background of the victim for any evidence that might develop a motive in the case.

- Inquire on whether or not the victim had insurance.
- Inquire as to where the insurance policies were located at the time of the fire.
- Inquire as to when the insurance was procured, and from what agent.

- Inquire as to whether there had been any recent increases in the amount of the insurance coverage.
- Inquire about any pending mortgages.
- Ascertain if the premium was paid recently.
- Obtain status of any loans on real property.
- Obtain status of any unpaid taxes.
- Obtain status of any chattel mortgages.
- Obtain status of any bankruptcy proceedings.
- Obtain status of any unpaid bills.
- Obtain status of any pending lawsuits.
- Ascertain if any statements, letters, or account books were opened to pages that the victim might have wanted destroyed.
- Check to see if the business was in the spouse's name and run a check on same for bankruptcy proceedings, insurance claims, and previous fires.

REVIEW QUESTIONS

1. What is arson?
2. What are the three classifications of arson? Give examples.
3. What is a pyromaniac?
4. What are the three causes of fires?
5. What are the elements that constitute the crime of arson?

11. Other Criminal Investigations

Larceny

Larceny is the wrongful taking, obtaining, or withholding by any means of money, personal property, or articles of value of any kind, from the possession of the true owner or of any other person in custody of the same, with the intent to permanently deprive or defraud another person of the use and benefit of such property.

Some examples of larceny are shoplifting, car theft, cargo theft, and fraud.

All the general principles of developing an investigation apply to larceny investigations (see *Criminal Investigations*). The private detective, while investigating a larceny, should:

- Determine time and date of the crime.
- Obtain a description and value of items taken.
- Determine who owned the property.
- Determine the location of the property at the time of the theft.
- Determine the details on how the crime was accomplished.
- Determine who knew the location and value of the property taken.
- Obtain facts pertaining to the description of the perpetrator.
- Search the scene for physical evidence.
- Interview witnesses and neighbors.

The solution of the crime of larceny must be proven beyond a reasonable doubt by competent and relevant evidence. The evidence must show that the accused wrongfully took, obtained, or withheld property from the possession of the true owner; that the property was of some value; and that the accused acted with intent to deprive or defraud the lawful owner of his property.

Burglary

Burglary is the unlawful entry of a building or occupied structure, or the surreptitious remaining in a building or occupied structure without having permission, with the intent to commit a crime therein. Unlawful entry into a house and taking some item from the house is burglary. Remaining in a store after it has closed to the public, taking some item from the store, and breaking out of the locked store is also considered burglary.

All the principles of developing an investigation apply to the burglary investigation (See *Criminal Investigations*). The private detective, while investigating a burglary, should:

- Determine the time and date of the crime.
- Determine the owner of the property.
- Obtain a description and value of items taken.
- Determine the details of how the crime was committed.
- Determine who knew the location and value of the items taken.
- Ascertain when the owners or occupants left the premises, where the keys were kept, who had access to the keys, and whether all doors and windows were secured.
- Search the scene for physical evidence.
- Interview witnesses and neighbors.

The solution of the crime of burglary must be proven beyond a reasonable doubt by competent and relevant evidence. Evidence must show that the accused unlawfully entered a building or occupied structure and did so with intent to commit a crime therein.

Robbery

Robbery is the taking, with intent to steal, anything of value from the person or in the presence of another against his will, by force or violence or fear of immediate or future injury to his person or property, or to persons or property of a relative, or of anyone in his company at the time of the robbery.

All principles on developing an investigation apply to the robbery investigation. The private detective, while investigating a robbery, should:

- Determine time and date of the crime.
- Determine victim's identity and extent of injuries.
- Obtain a description of perpetrator.
- Obtain a description and value of items taken.
- Determine if a weapon was used.
- Determine details on how the crime was accomplished.
- Interview witnesses and neighbors.
- Search the scene for physical evidence.

The solution of the crime of robbery must be proven beyond a reasonable doubt by competent and relevant evidence. The evidence must show that the accused wrongfully took, using force, threat of force or violence, from the possession of the true owner, or from the custody of a person, that the property was of some value, and that the accused acted with intent to deprive the lawful owner of his property.

Assault

An assault is an attempt or offer with unlawful force or violence to do bodily harm to another, whether or not the attempt or offer is consummated. An aggravated assault is an attempt to cause serious bodily injury to another, or cause such injury purposely, knowingly or recklessly, with or without a weapon.

All principles of developing an investigation apply to the assault investigation. The private detective, while investigating an assault, should:

- Determine time and date of the crime.
- Determine victim's identity and extent of injuries.
- Obtain a description of the offender.
- Determine the purpose of the crime.
- Determine the complete facts and circumstances surrounding the crime.
- Determine who else or what else was involved.
- Interview the victim, witnesses, and neighbors.
- Search the scene for physical evidence.

The solution of the crime of assault must be proven beyond a reasonable doubt by competent and relevant evidence. The evidence must show that the accused attempted or offered with unlawful force to do bodily harm to such person, and in the case of a consummated assault, the accused did bodily harm to such person with a certain weapon, unlawful force, or violence.

Sexual Assault

Sexual assault is the unlawful act of sexual penetration with another person. The act must be committed with a person under the lawful age or with any person where force or threat of violence is used.

All principles on developing an investigation apply to the sexual assault investigation. The private detective, while investigating a sexual assault case, should:

- Determine the time and date of the crime.
- Determine the victim's identity and extent of injuries.
- Obtain a description of the offender.
- Determine the complete facts and circumstances surrounding the crime.
- Interview the victim, witnesses, and neighbors.
- Search the scene for physical evidence.
- Discreetly obtain information concerning the reputation of the victim.
- Arrange for an immediate physical examination of the victim.
- Obtain the results from the medical examination.

The solution of the crime of sexual assault must be proven beyond a reasonable doubt by competent and relevant evidence. The evidence must show that the accused sexually penetrated the victim and that the victim was under the legal age, or that the accused sexually penetrated the victim by force or threat of violence.

Extortion

Extortion is the unlawful act of obtaining some property from a person by means of threatening to inflict bodily injury or exposing or publicizing to the public any secret or asserted fact, whether true or false, tending to subject a person to hatred, contempt, or ridicule.

All principles of developing an investigation apply to the extortion investigation. The private detective, while investigating an extortion, should:

- Determine the time and date of the crime.
- Determine the victim's identity.
- Obtain a description of the offender.
- Determine the complete facts and circumstances surrounding the crime.

- Determine the means of the crime.
- Determine who would benefit from the crime.
- Interview all parties concerned.

The solution of the crime of extortion must be proven beyond a reasonable doubt by competent and relevant evidence. The evidence must show that the accused obtained some property from a person by means of threatening to inflict bodily harm or by exposing or publicizing to the public any secret or asserted fact, whether true or false, tending to subject a person to hatred, contempt, or ridicule.

Forgery

Forgery is the false making or altering, with intent to defraud, any writing which would, if genuine, apparently impose legal liability or change the legal rights of another.

All principles of developing an investigation apply to forgery investigations. (See *Criminal Investigations*). The private detective, while investigating a forgery should:

- Determine time and date of the crime.
- Determine the victim's identity.
- Determine the purpose of the crime.
- Determine the complete facts and circumstances surrounding the crime.
- Determine the means of the crime.
- Determine who would benefit from the crime.
- Determine who had access to the documents or to the secret information.
- Obtain handwriting specimens for expert examination.
- Interview all parties concerned.

The solution of the crime of forgery must be proven beyond a reasonable doubt by competent and relevant evidence. The evidence must show that the accused falsely made or altered, with intent to defraud, any writing which would, if genuine, impose legal liability or change the rights of another.

Perjury

Perjury is the willful and corrupt giving, in any official proceeding and under a lawful oath or equivalent affirmation, of any false testimony material to the issue or matter of inquiry.

All principles on developing an investigation apply to the per-jury investigation. The private detective, while investigating a per-jury case, should:

- Determine time and date of the crime.
- Determine the complete facts and circumstances surrounding the crime.
- Interview all parties concerned.
- Obtain documentary proof that the testimony given was false.
- Determine the purpose of the crime.
- Obtain a copy of the transcript of the testimony in question. If it is not available, obtain written statements from witnesses who were present at the time the testimony was given.

The solution of the crime of perjury must be proven beyond a reasonable doubt by competent and relevant evidence. The evidence must show that the accused willfully and corruptly gave false testimony, while under a lawful oath, in an official proceeding.

Embezzlement

Embezzlement is the fraudulent appropriation of entrusted property or money. An employee who steals entrusted merchandise and a bank teller who takes money entrusted to him are examples of people practicing embezzlement.

All principles of developing an investigation apply to the embezzlement investigation. The private detective, while investigating an embezzlement case, should:

- Determine time and date of the crime.
- Determine victim's identity.
- Determine the purpose of the crime.
- Determine the complete facts and circumstances surroundng the crime.
- Determine who had access to the area where the missing items were kept.
- Determine who had custody of the missing items.
- Interview all parties concerned.

The solution of the crime of embezzlement must be proven beyond a reasonable doubt by competent and relevant evidence. The evidence must show that the accused fraudulently appropriated the entrusted property or money.

Drugs

The misuse of drugs can be observed in the affluent society as well as in the slums. Drugs show no barrier to race, color, creed, or status in society. Drugs are taking their toll in the schools, in business, and in every other type of enterprise that one can think of. Because drugs are very much a part of our society, the private detective should know about them. In many cases that a private detective will be investigating, drugs could be involved.

For instance, in theft cases, the perpetrator may have stolen items so that he could buy drugs. Or in accident cases, the person involved in the accident may have been on drugs. In homicide cases, the perpetrator may have committed murder because he was double-crossed in a drug buy, or he wanted to steal money or drugs from the victim. And in missing person cases, the reason the person is missing may be that he is on drugs and wants to get away from everyone that he knows.

Drugs can either be of an addicting nature or of a habit-forming nature. Addiction means that the body craves and needs a drug. It is a physical dependency. Habit forming means a mental craving. It is a psychological dependency.

Drugs can be divided into four areas:

1. Narcotics
2. Depressants
3. Stimulants
4. Hallucinogens

Narcotics produce insensibility or a stupor due to their depressant effect on the central nervous system and are addicting.

Opium in its natural state is the milky white sap from the poppy, which is grown in Asia, the Middle East, and in Latin America. Upon exposure to air, it turns to a dark brown gumlike substance. In the laboratory, the opium gum is boiled with a mixture of water and glycerine until the water is evaporated. The remaining product is prepared opium and is ready for use. The prepared opium can be smoked in a pipe, chewed, swallowed, or drunk as opium wine. Opium is addicting and causes euphoria, relaxation, and grandiose dreams. Use of this drug can cause death, loss of appetite, constipation, loss of sex drive, or loss of productive drive. *Mud, tar, black stuff, hop,* and *op* are all slang terms for opium.

Morphine is an extract of raw opium. After processing the opium in the laboratory, the substance becomes morphine, which is a white crystalline powder and is extremely bitter to the taste. Morphine can be swallowed or injected and causes the same effects as opium. Use of this drug can cause death, constipation, nausea, and loss of appetite. *White stuff, morph, dreamer, Miss Emma,* and *M* are all slang terms for morphine.

Heroin is the trade name of a drug obtained from opium. After processing, the opium product becomes heroin and is a white or off-white crystalline powder. Heroin can be injected, sniffed, or smoked, and causes the same effects as opium. Use of this drug can cause death, constipation, or loss of appetite. *Scag, H, horse, junk, smack, stuff,* and *harry* are all slang terms for heroin.

Cocaine is a product of the coca plant that grows in Formosa, Java, and South America. After processing, the substance becomes cocaine, which is a white and fluffy crystalline powder. Cocaine can be sniffed, injected, or swallowed, and causes excitation and euphoria. Use of this drug can cause depression, convulsions, and psychosis. *Coke, C, Snow, dust,* and *flake* are all slang terms for cocaine.

Crack is a smokable form of cocaine. Smoking this drug allows large amounts of it to reach the brain quickly and produces a more intense and rapid high. Use of this drug can cause confusion, anxiety, psychological problems, and even death.

Depressants are synthetic drugs that depress the central nervous system to relieve tension or produce sleep, and are addicting.

Barbiturates are synthetic drugs that are manufactured by pharmaceutical companies for the medical profession. People misuse this drug because it causes euphoria and reduced anxiety. In tablet or capsule form, it is taken orally or injected. The use of this type of drug can cause death, mental confusion, severe withdrawal, or seizures. *Downers, goof balls, candy, red devils,* and *yellow devils* are all slang terms for barbiturates.

Tranquilizers are synthetic drugs that are manufactured by pharmaceutical companies for the medical profession. People misuse this drug because it causes euphoria and reduces anxiety. In tablet or powder form, it can be taken orally or injected, and use of this drug can affect the kidneys or cause a coma.

Stimulants are drugs that stimulate the central nervous system. They produce a feeling of excitement and are habit forming.

Amphetamines are synthetic drugs that are manufactured by pharmaceutical companies for the medical profession. People misuse this drug because it improves alertness, reduces fatigue, and causes euphoria. In tablet, capsule, liquid, or powder form, it is taken orally or injected. The use of this drug can cause loss of appetite, delusions, or hallucinations. *Ups, uppers, pep pills,* and *wake-ups* are all slang terms for amphetamines.

Hallucinogens are drugs that produce dreamlike images and hallucinations and are habit forming.

Marijuana is a hallucinogenic drug consisting of the leaves of the Indian hemp plant that have been dried and ground up. The finished product can be smoked in a pipe, rolled into a cigarette and smoked, swallowed, or chewed. It causes euphoria, relaxation, and increased perception. Use of this drug can cause psychosis, impaired coordination, and conjunctivitis. *Weed, pot, grass, hay, joint,* and *Mary Jane* are all slang terms for marijuana.

Hashish is the raw resin extracted from the tops of the Indian hemp plant. The resin is reduced to powder form and kneaded into sticks or chunks. The finished product can be smoked or swallowed. It causes the same effects as marijuana. *Hash* is the slang term for hashish.

LSD is an experimental synthetic drug. Its official name is D-Lysergic Acid Diethylamide, and was produced for experimental use only in the possible control of psychological problems. Unfortunately, it is now being produced illegally. In tablet, capsule, or liquid form, it is either swallowed or injected. The drug can increase insight and cause exhilaration. The side effects of the drug range from panic reactions to continuous flashbacks. *Acid, big D, sugar, cubes,* and *trips* are all slang terms for LSD.

PCP is another hallucinogenic drug. Phencyclidine is the official name of this illegally produced synthetic drug. Sold on the streets as tablets, powder, pills, or crystals, this drug can be swallowed or smoked and produces a floating, euphoric high. Use of the drug can cause convulsions, coma, or even death. *Angel dust* is the slang term for PCP.

Aside from marijuana smokers, very few people use drugs openly. Observation is made more difficult because of this. However, it is of importance to remember that contacts between the addict and the peddler for the exchange of money and drugs are made on the street or in public places such as restaurants, bars, bus terminals, railroad stations, and theaters. In observing the activities of addicts or suspected addicts, the private detective should note the persons whom they meet, where they meet, and the places they visit. In most cases, addicts tend to repeat their patterns and will hang around the same corner or go to the same house predictably.

By watching a drug addict, the private detective may be able to furnish the clue to the identity of the pusher who is supplying the addict. It frequently happens that the addict himself is also a peddler. Observation of his actions will lead to the detection of other addicts and more important, to the source of supply for the addict-seller. Observation of a drug addict or seller will also lead to the detection of other persons engaged in this illegal activity, since most of their contacts are maintained on an individual basis, one leading to another.

Drug users will carefully conceal drugs and related paraphernalia so as not to be discovered. Drug paraphernalia could include teaspoons, hypodermic syringes, medicine or eye droppers, empty gelatin capsules, scales, measuring spoons, pipes, and strainers. Drugs and related paraphernalia can be hidden in:

- Fountain pens
- Cigarette holders and lighters
- Trouser lining at the waistband
- Pinned on the inside of necktie
- Pinned on the inside of trouser fly
- Pinned on the inside leg of pants or coat sleeve
- Secured to leg, thigh, or arm by means of rubberband or adhesive tape
- Wrapped in balloons and secreted in cavities of the body
- Hatband, inside or outside
- Chewing gum or cigarette packages
- Tobacco cans (under paper that separates tobacco from metal)
- The lining of coats and cuffs of pants
- Bedposts, mattresses, waste baskets, and tissue boxes
- Behind pictures, light fixtures, baseboards, holes in the wall, medicine cabinets, garbage cans, taped to the bottom or upper frames of dresser

REVIEW QUESTIONS

1. What is the meaning of:
- Larceny?
- Burglary?
- Robbery?
- Assault?
- Sexual assault?
- Extortion?
- Forgery?
- Perjury?
- Embezzlement?

2. How is drug use tied into the major types of crime?

3. What are the four classifications of drugs? Give examples.

12. Divorce Investigation

Divorce investigation is another type of civil case that the private detective will be involved with. Divorce is the legal separation of a husband and wife, effective for cause, by the judgment of a court and totally dissolving the marriage relation.

Types of Divorces

Each of the states, along with the District of Columbia, Virgin Islands, and Puerto Rico, has its own set of divorce laws. Depending on the jurisdiction, divorce can be classified as a fault divorce or a no-fault divorce. A *no-fault divorce* is the dissolution of a marriage upon the showing that the marriage is irretrievably broken or has irreconcilable differences. Basically, both parties of the marriage are unable to or refuse to cohabit, and there are no prospects of any kind of reconciliation. The parties to the marriage must convince the court that the marriage is ended because of the basic unsuitability of the spouses to each other and their states of mind toward the relationship. By the very nature of this type of divorce, there is no investigative work for the private detective.

A *fault divorce* is the dissolution of a marriage whereby one of the parties to the marriage has to prove one or more of the grounds for divorce as provided for in state law. Specific laws for all state jurisdictions are covered later in this chapter. Grounds for a fault divorce vary from jurisdiction to jurisdiction. Adultery, bigamy, drug addiction, insanity, felony conviction, imprisonment, incest, alcohol addiction, nonsupport, neglect, legal separation, and extreme cruelty are examples of grounds for divorce. If the fault is substantiated by proof, the court could grant a divorce. Thus, the gathering of proof in the fault divorce could be a task for the private detective.

Adultery Investigation

Adultery is voluntary sexual intercourse between two unrelated men and women, at least one of whom is married. Most divorce cases that a private detective will take on will involve adultery. In order to prove adultery, opportunity and inclination must be proved.

Opportunity simply implies a convenient time and place; i.e., a good chance to commit adultery. Opportunity may be proven by evidence showing that at the time of the alleged adultery, the defendant had ample time to accomplish his desires. Being alone with the third party in any place such as a private room, auto, hotel, or any unfrequented place will usually be accepted as proof of opportunity. A visit of a married person to a known house of prostitution, or association with a prostitute, will justify the assumption that such visits are for improper purposes.

Inclination is the tendency to favor one person over another. Inclination may be shown by expressions of affection either spoken or written, photographs of the subject and another party in affectionate poses, or photographs with affectionate inscriptions. Frequent and unexplained absences from home on the part of the subject, and false statements to the plaintiff, may all go to build up this aspect of the investigation. Solicitation of sexual intercourse by the defendant may be admissible in court as showing inclination toward adultery.

The first step of an adultery investigation occurs when the private detective is approached by a client to investigate the activities of his or her spouse. At this point, the private detective must decide on whether or not to take the case. If he does, he must obtain from the client all pertinent information needed to complete an investigation. The use of the background report is essential. A photograph of the subject must be obtained for positive identification (see chapter on *Developing Leads*).

The next step is to set up a surveillance schedule that will allow the private detective to gain evidence for the client. This evidence can be either photographic or in the form of your first-hand testimony (see chapter on *Surveillance*).

Remember, the days of the private detective kicking down the motel room door are over. It is against the law for a private detective to do so, and he will be charged with felony burglary. All the private detective has to prove is opportunity and inclination on the part of the person being investigated. Your photographers and/or your testimony will undoubtedly be used in civil court. At this time, you will be ordered to testify and produce all evidence pertinent to the case.

Notes should be kept by the private detective while on divorce surveillances. After the private detective has completed his investigation, a formal typewritten report can be completed from the notes taken during the investigation. The notes should tell:

- Times and dates when the surveillance was started and completed.
- Exact times and dates of all events that take place.
- Exact locations of areas under surveillance and the routes of travel.
- Exact description of subject under surveillance and the vehicle used. *I*
- Exact description of persons being met by the subject, the time and date, as well as the location of the meeting.

Bigamy Investigation

Bigamy is a willful and knowing contract of marriage while being married to a third party. It is grounds for divorce in several states. On occasion, the private detective will be investigating this type of fault for a client. If one party to the marriage has another spouse, it is up to the private detective to find out all of the pertinent facts. The most effective way to prove bigamy is for the private detective to follow the suspected spouse. It may be a long process, but sooner or later the subject will go to the other spouse.

Once the location of the second home and family has been established, the private detective must find out the name that the subject is living under. Interviewing neighbors will establish this. To prove bigamy, the private detective must show that the subject is married to the third party. Marriage records are kept on both the local and state levels. The private detective must obtain a copy of the marriage certificate.

Extreme Cruelty

Extreme cruelty is also grounds for divorce in several states, and concerns the conduct or treatment of one spouse towards the other. The conduct must be malicious, intended to force a separation, and dangerous to the life or health of the spouse (mental or physical health). In handling such a case, the private detective must gather proof that can be used in a court of law. Statements from the victim, neighbors, and witnesses can supply all the proof that is needed for a lawyer to establish extreme cruelty. It would help the case if the private detective also obtained statements and documentary evidence from the victim's doctor and/or psychiatrist.

Alcohol or Drug Addiction

Another type of grounds for divorce in many states is alcohol and/or drug addiction. The establishment of proof in most such addiction cases can be easy. If the spouse in question practices his addiction in the open, the private detective need only interview the neighbors and other witnesses and then submit their statements as proof. If the subject hides the addiction, the private detective must follow the subject to the location where the addiction is practiced so that proof can be established. Witnessing the subject drinking alcohol excessively and frequently, buying drugs, or consorting in known drug circles are all examples of the types of proof that a private detective must establish here.

Grounds for Divorce

Following are synopses of each state's respective laws that define legal grounds for divorce.

Alabama

Irreconcilable differences, adultery, bigamy, desertion, impotency, abandonment, felony conviction or imprisonment, alcohol or drug addiction, insanity, or fraud, force, and duress.

Alaska

Desertion, drug or alcohol addiction, adultery, insanity, felony conviction or imprisonment, bigamy, extreme cruelty, and impotency.

Arizona

Irretrievably broken (no-fault).

Arkansas

Bigamy, desertion, impotency, adultery, insanity, nonsupport, separation or absence, felony conviction or imprisonment, alcohol or drug addiction, and extreme cruelty.

California
Irreconcilable differences (no-fault) and insanity.

Colorado
Irreconcilable differences (no fault), bigamy, fraud, force, duress, impotency, and insanity.

Connecticut
Irreconcilable differences (no-fault), extreme cruelty, adultery, separation or absence, insanity, felony conviction or imprisonment, fraud, force, duress, alcohol addiction, and impotency.

Delaware
Irretrievably broken (no-fault), drug addiction, bigamy, fraud, force, duress, impotency, and insanity.

Florida
Irreconcilable differences (no-fault) and insanity.

Georgia
Irreconcilable differences (no-fault), separation or absence, adultery, bigamy, insanity, impotency, incest, extreme cruelty, fraud, force, duress, and alcohol or drug addiction.

Hawaii
Irreconcilable differences (no-fault), separation or absence, bigamy, impotency, fraud, force, and duress.

Idaho
Irreconcilable differences (no-fault), separation or absence, adultery, extreme cruelty, insanity, felony conviction or imprisonment, impotency, neglect, alcoholism, bigamy, non-support or fraud, force, and duress.

Illinois
Adultery, bigamy, alcohol or drug addiction, felony conviction or imprisonment, desertion, extreme cruelty, and impotency.

Indiana
Irreconcilable differences (no-fault), insanity, felony conviction or imprisonment, impotency, bigamy, fraud, force, and duress.

Iowa
Marriage breakdown (no-fault), bigamy, impotency, and insanity.

Kansas
Insanity, alcohol addiction, adultery, separation or absence,

extreme cruelty, felony conviction or imprisonment, impotency, nonsupport, bigamy or fraud, force, and duress.

Kentucky
Irreconcilable differences (no-fault) and impotency.

Louisiana
Adultery, separation, felony conviction or imprisonment, and bigamy.

Maine
Irreconcilable differences (no-fault), extreme cruelty, adultery, separation or absence, alcohol or drug addiction, insanity, impotency, nonsupport, and felony conviction or imprisonment.

Maryland
Adultery, separation or absence, felony conviction or imprisonment, impotency, and bigamy.

Massachusetts
Irreconcilable differences (no-fault), impotency, fraud, force or duress, nonsupport, alcohol addiction, extreme cruelty, adultery, separation or absence, neglect, felony conviction or imprisonment, and bigamy.

Michigan
Breakdown of marriage (no-fault) and bigamy.

Minnesota
Irreconcilable differences (no-fault), fraud, force, and duress.

Mississippi
Drug or alcohol addiction, extreme cruelty, adultery, impotency, insanity, separation or absence, incest, bigamy, felony conviction or imprisonment, fraud, force, and duress.

Missouri
Irreconcilable differences (no-fault), bigamy, separation or absence, impotency, fraud, force, and duress.

Montana
Irreconcilable differences (no-fault), bigamy, fraud, force, and duress.

Nebraska
Irreconcilable differences (no-fault).

Nevada
Irreconcilable differences (no-fault), insanity, separation or absence, nonsupport or fraud, force, and duress.

New Hampshire
Irreconcilable differences (no-fault), adultery, separation or absence, extreme cruelty, nonsupport, impotency, felony conviction or imprisonment, and alcohol abuse.

New Jersey
Separation or absence, adultery, deviant sexual conduct, alcohol or drug addiction, extreme cruelty, impotency, insanity, bigamy, felony conviction or imprisonment, fraud, force, and duress.

New Mexico
Irreconcilable differences, adultery, extreme cruelty, separation or absence, and incompatibility.

New York
Adultery, separation or absence, extreme cruelty, felony conviction or imprisonment, deviant sexual conduct, and mutual consent.

North Carolina
Impotency, adultery, separation or absence, insanity, and unnatural sexual acts.

North Dakota
Irreconcilable differences (no-fault), separation or absence, bigamy, adultery, extreme cruelty, insanity, felony conviction or imprisonment, fraud, force, and duress.

Ohio
Adultery, bigamy, separation or absence, extreme cruelty, impotency, alcohol addiction, felony conviction or imprisonment, nonsupport, insanity, mutal consent, fraud, force, and duress.

Oklahoma
Extreme cruelty, adultery, separation or absence, impotency, felony conviction or imprisonment, alcohol addiction, nonsupport, insanity, fraud, force, and duress.

Oregon
Irreconcilable differences (no-fault), fraud, force, and duress.

Pennsylvania
Irreconcilable differences (no-fault), adultery, bigamy, impotency,

extreme cruelty, separation or absence, felony conviction or imprisonment, incest, insanity, mutual consent, fraud, force, and duress.

Rhode Island
Irreconcilable differences (no-fault), adultery, impotency, alcohol or drug addiction, extreme cruelty, bigamy, and nonsupport.

South Carolina
Separation or absence, adultery, alcohol or drug addiction, and extreme cruelty.

South Dakota
Separation or absence, adultery, extreme cruelty, felony conviction or imprisonment, impotency, insanity, bigamy, fraud, force, and duress.

Tennessee
Irreconcilable differences (no-fault), impotency, separation or absence, adultery, bigamy, felony conviction or imprisonment, alcohol or drug addiction, extreme cruelty, nonsupport, fraud, force, and duress.

Texas
Irreconcilable differences (no-fault), separation or absence, adultery, extreme cruelty, felony conviction or imprisonment, insanity, alcohol or drug addiction, bigamy, fraud, force, and duress.

Utah
Adultery, impotency, separation or absence, alcohol addiction, felony conviction or imprisonment, extreme cruelty, insanity, bigamy, nonsupport, fraud, force, and duress.

Vermont
Adultery, felony conviction or imprisonment, separation or absence, insanity, and nonsupport.

Virginia
Separation or absence, adultery, unnatural sexual activity, felony conviction or imprisonment, bigamy, extreme cruelty, and impotency.

Washington
Irreconcilable differences (no-fault).

West Virginia
Irreconcilable differences (no-fault), adultery, alcohol or drug addiction, felony conviction or imprisonment, extreme cruelty, insanity, impotency, bigamy, and separation or absence.

Wisconsin
Irreconcilable differences (no-fault), separation or absence, bigamy, impotency, fraud, force, and duress.

Wyoming
Irreconcilable differences (no-fault) and bigamy.

District of Columbia
Bigamy, separation or absence, insanity, fraud, force, and duress.

Virgin Islands
Irreconcilable differences (no-fault) or bigamy.

Puerto Rico
Separation or absence, adultery, extreme cruelty, impotency, insanity, fraud, force, and duress.

REVIEW QUESTIONS

1. What is the definition of divorce?
2. What are the two types of divorce? What are the differences?
3. What is adultery? What must be proven in an adultery case?
4. What is bigamy? What type of proof is needed to establish bigamy?

13. Other Civil Investigations

LOCATING MISSING PERSONS

Many times the private detective will be approached to locate a person who is missing. Lawyers, concerned family members or friends, and businesses are always trying to locate people for a variety of reasons. Lawyers are involved in many lawsuits where one or more of the parties and or witnesses cannot be found. Also, in some divorce cases, one parent will take the children and disappear before the case goes to court and the custody of the children is granted. Family members and friends will approach the private detective to locate a loved one. This type of missing person could be a juvenile runaway, a disgruntled spouse, or a person with psychological problems. Finally, businesses are concerned with locating people who owe them money and have disappeared.

Investigation Techniques

The success or failure of this type of investigation will depend largely upon the type and amount of information obtained from the client concerning the missing person. The background report (See *Developing Leads*) is an invaluable tool for the private detective. Basically, it is a checklist for the needed information that must be gathered and then followed up on. The private detective must obtain the maximum amount of information about the subject. Each bit of information is a potential lead that could reveal the location of the missing person. When conducting the initial interview, the private detective should never rely upon his memory. All information should be recorded in the background report.

106

The private detective should always obtain a recent photograph of the subject. This will prove to be invaluable in making a positive identification. Just as important is a full and detailed physical description of the subject. The description should include:

- *Height*
- *Build*—stout, medium, thin, erect, stooping, etc.
- *Complexion*—smooth, pale, fair, dark, clear, makeup, etc.
- *Face*—round, long broad, wrinkled, etc.
- *Facial hair*—beard, moustache, goatee, clean shaven, etc.
- *Hair*—color, quantity, style, waved, curled, bleached, dyed, receding, etc.
- *Nose*—large, small, straight, flat, turned up, long, wide, etc.
- *Chin*—projecting, double, dimpled, etc.
- *Forehead*—low, high, straight, bulging, etc.
- *Eyebrows*—color, thin, thick, shape, etc.
- *Eyes*—glasses, color, large, small peculiarities, etc.
- *Mouth*—large, small, drooping, etc.
- *Teeth*—missing, color, dentures, condition, peculiarities, etc.
- *Ears*—large, small, long, short, close to head, protruding, etc.
- *Cheeks*—full, bony, fleshy, flat, sunken, etc.
- *Head*—round, flat, egg-shaped, etc.
- *Neck*—short, long curved, straight, fat, thin, etc.
- *Lips*—thick, thin, protruding, etc.
- *Distinguishing marks*—scars, birthmarks, warts, tattoos, pimples, etc.
- *Peculiarities*—accent, speech, deformities, etc.

The private detective must not forget that the missing person may have altered his appearance to hide his identity. The following methods may be used by the subject to alter his appearance:

- Growing a moustache or beard if he had none formally or shaving it off if he had one.
- Wearing glasses if none were formally worn or discarding them if previously worn.
- Dyeing his hair or skin.
- Destroying original tattoo marks by having them covered or altered with other patterns.
- Changing gold fillings on the front teeth, capping teeth, or changing the contour of the face by using dentures.

- Altering distinctive characteristics of the face, such as scars, moles, nose, lips, and ears by plastic surgery.
- Altering the appearance of the eyes in respect to size and shape by having a surgical operation performed on the eyelids.

After obtaining the necessary background information, investigate the residence where the subject lived and where the subject worked. Information gathered at these locations can reveal the possible destination of the subject as well as possible friends or associates of the subject. The private detective should collect anything and everything that the subject wrote down, including names, addresses, telephone numbers, letters, and so on. Also, check prior telephone bills for toll calls. The bill might contain a long distance phone call and that location may be where the subject is. Finally, if the disappearance is recent, the private detective should go through the subject's garbage and try to find any notations or literature that could be connected with the subject and his new location.

After all of the background information is collected, the private detective should analyze all of the collected data and then organize it in such a manner that all leads can be pursued in a logical and orderly manner.

AUTOMOBILE ACCIDENT INVESTIGATION

An accident is an event that causes loss, injury, or death resulting from carelessness, ignorance, or unavoidable causes. The majority of the accident cases that will be investigated by the private detective will be connected with automobile accidents.

An automobile accident is a collision involving an automobile and one of the following:

1. Another automobile or automobiles.
2. A pedestrian.
3. An animal.
4. A fixed object such as a telephone pole, building or sign.
5. Another type of vehicle other than an automobile; i.e., a bus, train, bicycle, or motorcycle.

Investigation Techniques

In cases involving an automobile accident, the private detective will use basically the same avenues of investigation as he would use for other investigations. The private detective's main objective is to provide evidence for the client that can be used in a court of law to provide for a settlement of the client's claim. It is up to the civil court to decide who was at fault and if any damages should be awarded.

The success or failure of the investigation depends largely upon the amount and quality of the initial information gathered. The detective should gather all of the available information that is at hand. After he is retained by the client, the background report should be completed and all information followed up on (see *Developing Leads*).

Next, the private detective should obtain a copy of the official police report. The report will contain information on victims, witnesses, causes, etcetera. Once obtained, a survey of the accident scene should be made. The scene should be photographed and any irregularities noted.

The interviewing of all victims, witnesses, doctors, and all other parties connected with the case is the next investigative step (see *Interview, Interrogation,* and *Report Writing*). If it is at all possible, the private detective should obtain signed statements.

Finally, the private detective should analyze all the information that has been gathered, and determine, through the evidence gathered, who was at fault.

PREEMPLOYMENT INQUIRY

Many businesses retain private detectives to perform background investigations on subjects being considered for employment, or for a current employee who is being considered for a promotion and has never had an inquiry made into his background. The purpose of this type of investigation is to verify the accuracy and completeness of statements made by the subject to the prospective employer, and to develop any additional information on the subject that could be useful to the prospective employer.

Investigative Techniques

The private detective should obtain a copy of the employment application and a copy of the subject's resume. To avoid any civil lawsuits resulting from invasion of privacy, the private detective should require a release form from the subject under investigation (see *Developing Leads*). This form will also open many files that are normally closed to the public.

The application and resume should contain all the necessary background data. Everything that is written down should be verified.

The following is a list of seven types of data that are needed from the subject under investigation, and the proper investigative steps that must be taken to complete the background inquiry:

1. *Personal data*—Obtain name, date of birth, place of birth, parent's name, marital status, and number of dependents. This data can be verified by checking the birth and marriage records which are kept at the city and/or state levels.
2. *Address*—Obtain current and previous addresses. This data can be verified by checking the county deed records and by interviewing neighbors who may know the subject.
3. *Education*—Obtain the names and addresses all schools attended including elementary, high school, colleges, and technical schools. This data can be verified by checking the records at each school the subject claims to have attended. It might be necessary to utilize the release form for gaining access to the files.
4. *Employment*—Obtain names and addresses of present and previous employers and the reasons for leaving. This data can be verified by direct contact with present and prior employers. The release form will be needed.
5. *References*—Obtain names and addresses of persons who have known the subject for a substantial period of time. Each reference must be interviewed about the character of the subject being investigated.
6. *Military service*—Obtain branch of service, period of service, type of discharge, and rank held. To verify this type of data, a release form will be needed. The government has restrictions on what type of information it can give out.
7. *Criminal history*—The Civil Rights Act of 1964 states that a question inquiring about prior arrests is illegal. However, it is permissible to ask about convictions. Before such a question is ever asked of an applicant, it would be necessary to check the state law because some state laws prohibit the asking of this question. The private detective can still make inquiries at local and state police bureaus. A release form will be necessary.

REVIEW QUESTIONS

1. What kind of information can be obtained from a search of the missing subject's residence?
2. How may a missing subject alter his appearance so as to hide his identity?
3. What purpose does the background information report serve?
4. What is the definition of an automobile accident?
5. What is the purpose of a preemployment inquiry?
6. In what instances is a release form needed in the procurement of personal information?

14. Starting Your Own Business

There are many points to consider when setting up your own private detective business. Only basic items are needed, and they are discussed in the following text. There is only one thing missing, and that is practical experience. Before starting his own business, a new private detective should first work for an established private detective agency where valuable knowledge and practical experience can be gained.

Compliance with the Law

The first chapter discussing the private detective and the law covers the various state laws that regulate this profession. One must always research the law and follow the proper procedures that are so set up. Failure to comply with the law will result in fines and/or imprisonment.

Insurance Coverage

There are three types of insurance coverage that a private detective should have: surety bond, professional liability, and Workmen's Compensation coverage. A surety bond, or good faith bond, is a policy by which the bonding company agrees to pay an agreed sum of money when the bonded person fails to perform his contractual agreement with a third party. This type of coverage is required in a majority of states which regulate the private detective business. Liability insurance is a policy by which the insurance company assumes the risk of liability for damage to the person or his property. Basically, this type of coverage is not required by state regulation of the private detective business. Workmen's compensation is a type of liability coverage for the compensation of workmen who are injured in the course of their employment. The laws vary from state to state, so it is best to check with your particular state.

Professional Assistance

The private detective will on occasion need the assistance of professional people from the legal and accounting field. The lawyer can handle any legal matters or legal questions that may arise. Due to the nature of the private detective business, it would be of great advantage to be on friendly terms with an attorney who may do you a favor by answering legal/investigative questions without charging a fee. Accountants are important for your financial well-being. They will prepare the proper tax returns, maintain your financial books, ensure that all tax deductions are included in your tax return, and provide advice on financial investments and planning.

The Office

The initial office expenses should be kept to a minimum. If it is at all possible, work out of your home. This will keep the overhead down. Obtain a desk, a file cabinet, a portable typewriter, and basic office supplies. To project a good image, a professional-looking business card and letterhead should be printed. A separate telephone should be exclusively utilized for business purposes. Finally, obtain a good dictionary of the English language and dictionary of law terms.

Advertising

The new private detective must spread the word that he is in business. One way is to place an ad in the yellow pages of the telephone book. There is a monthly charge for this ad, and it could give your new business a wide exposure to the public and to professional people looking for your talents. Since you will be working for lawyers, an ad can be taken in your state's law journal. Here, one has the maximum exposure to the legal field. Finally, direct mail can be utilized. Direct mail is the sending of advertising material to specific persons or businesses. The literature that you send out should describe the professional services that you offer. The mailing piece should be professionally written and printed, if your budget will allow it.

Investigative Equipment

The camera, both still and moving, is an excellent tool for the private detective. Photos can save you time from writing descriptive passages in your reports. They can also preserve the presence of items that would undoubtedly be moved from their original state. The camera can also be used in surveillance operations. You might buy a good telephoto lens which will make long distances seem close.

An elaborate crime lab is not needed by the private detective. This type of equipment is very expensive. The private detective should obtain a fingerprint impression/lifting kit. This equipment can be purchased from law enforcement supply houses.

The tape recorder is another important tool for the private detective. They come in a variety of sizes and shapes. The small pocket recorders are used to record material from an undercover or clandestine situation. The desk size recorder can be used for recording statements and dictation. Finally, the private detective will need a telephone answering machine which will answer all calls when he is out of the office.

Another important item for the private detective is a pair of binoculars. Binoculars are needed when on any kind of surveillance operation. The cost is minimal, but your return can be maximal.

The private detective must consider whether or not he is going to carry a gun. A weapons permit must be obtained from the state. Then you will be entitled to carry a concealed weapon. The type of work you wish to pursue will determine the type of firearms that you will need. The general private detective can do without a weapon, but once a private detective starts working within the heavy criminal scene, a handgun is needed.

If you plan on doing bodyguard or executive protection type work, a larger arsenal consisting of handguns, rifles, and shotguns might be necessary. First, decide what type of work you will be doing, and then consult a reputable licensed firearms dealer for advice.

Investigator's Ethics

The private detective's career is a highly technical and a highly professional one. Doctors, lawyers, and law enforcement personnel are bound by their own particular codes of ethics.

A code of ethics can best be described as: The values or principles of conduct which govern members of a profession among themselves and with all other persons encountered while acting in their professional capacity.

PRIVATE DETECTIVE'S CODE OF ETHICS

1. To perform investigations in a professional, moral, and ethical manner.
2. To work within the framework of the law.
3. To maintain the highest standards when in the process of investigating.
4. To help maintain law and order by bringing to justice anyone who has broken the law.
5. To conduct investigations for a lawful use.
6. To protect confidential information.
7. To tell the whole truth when presenting evidence.

REVIEW QUESTIONS

1. What are the three basic types of insurance coverage a private investigator should have? Explain each type.
2. What type of investigative equipment is needed for the private detective profession?
3. What is a code of ethics? What is the private detective's code of ethics?

Glossary

Accident—An event that causes loss or injury resulting from carelessness, ignorance, or unavoidable causes.

Addiction—A physical dependency where the body craves and needs a drug.

Adultery—Voluntary sexual intercourse between two parties, one of whom is married.

Aggravated Assault—An attempt, either successful or unsuccessful, to cause serious bodily injury to another knowingly, or recklessly, with or without a weapon.

Amphetamine—A synthetic stimulant drug that can be taken orally or injected, and is habit forming. Can cause death, loss of appetite, delusions, and hallucinations.

Arrest—The act of depriving a person of his freedom; to take into custody for an unlawful act.

Arson—The willful and malicious burning of property.

Assault—An attempt or offer to do bodily harm to another with unlawful force or violence, whether or not the attempt or offer is consummated.

Attempt—Any act done with intent to commit a crime, but failing to effect its commission.

Barbiturate—A synthetic depressant drug that can be taken orally or injected and is addicting. Can cause death, mental confusion, severe withdrawal, and seizures. See "Depressant"

Bigamy—Willfully and knowingly contracting a marriage while being married to a third party.

117

Burglary—Breaking and entering into a building with intent to commit a felony.

Circumstantial Evidence—That evidence which in itself does not directly prove the fact at issue, but establishes a certain fact or series of facts which tend to prove certain elements of the case or question. Also called indirect evidence.

Civil Law—That area of law which concerns the rights and obligations people have in their relations with one another.

Cocaine—A narcotic drug that is produced from the coca plant. Can be sniffed, injected, or swallowed and is addicting. Can cause death, depression, convulsions, and psychosis.

Common Law—Principles and rules of action which derive their authority solely from usages and customs from the judgments and decrees of the courts, recognizing, affirming, and enforcing such usages and customs.

Competent Evidence—Evidence which is qualified, reliable, and suitable for the case in point.

Confession—A voluntary statement made by a person charged with a crime, wherein he acknowledges himself to be guilty of the offense charged.

Conspiracy—Agreement between two or more persons to do an unlawful act in an unlawful manner, or to do a lawful act in an unlawful way.

Corpus Delicti—The body of the crime; the substantial fact that a crime has been committed.

Crack—A narcotic drug that is a form of cocaine. This drug is smoked and produces an intense and rapid high. Use of this drug can cause confusion, anxiety, psychological problems, and death.

Crime—An act or omission forbidden by law.

Criminal Intent—State of mind directed toward the committing of some unlawful act.

Defamation—Damage done to the reputation of a person. Can either be written (libel) or spoken (slander).

Depressants—Synthetic drugs that depress the central nervous system to relieve tension or to produce sleep. Addicting in nature. Barbiturates and tranquilizers are depressants.

Direct Evidence—Evidence which tends to show the existence of the facts in question which a witness draws from his own personal knowledge; derived through one or more of his five senses.

Divorce—Legal separation of a husband and wife, effected for cause by the judgment of a court, and totally dissolving the marriage relation.

Duress—When a person is forced or compelled to do a criminal act by another.

Dying Declaration—Written or verbal statement made by a mortally wounded person who knows that he is about to die, and has abandoned all hope of recovery.

Embezzlement—The fraudulent appropriation of entrusted property or money.

Evidence—That which demonstrates, makes clear, or ascertains the truth of the very fact or point in issue, either on the one side or the other. That which makes a fact evident. That which supplies proof. The means by which any point may be proved or disproved.

Extortion—The unlawful act of obtaining some property from another by means of threatening to inflict bodily injury, or exposing to the public any secret or asserted fact, whether true or false, tending to subject a person to hatred, contempt, or ridicule.

Eyewitness—A person who can testify as to what he has seen.

Fault Divorce—The dissolution of a marriage where one of the parties to the marriage has to prove one or more of the grounds for divorce as provided for in the law that covers the jurisdiction in question.

Felony—A crime of very serious nature.

Fixed Surveillance—Secret observation of persons, places, or things from a fixed position so as to obtain information.

Forgery—The false making or material altering, with intent to defraud, any writing which would, if genuine, apparently impose legal inability or change the legal rights of another.

Habit Forming—A psychological dependency for a drug; a mental craving.

Hallucinogen—Drug that produces dream images or hallucinations and is habit forming. Marijuana, hashish, and LSD are all hallucinogens.

Hashish—A hallucinogenic drug that is extracted from the tops of the Indian Hemp plant. Can be smoked or swallowed and is habit forming. Can cause psychosis, impaired coordination, and conjunctivitis.

Hearsay Evidence—Evidence which was not gained through a person's senses; usually not admissible in court.

Heroin—A narcotic drug that is produced from opium. It can be injected, sniffed, or smoked and is addicting. Can cause death, constipation, and loss of appetite.

Homicide—The killing of a human being by another.

Incendiary Fire—A fire that was maliciously and willfully set.

Indirect Evidence—Evidence drawn from inferences and assumptions, or those things which would indicate that a person could have committed the act, or was in the position to have done so.

Informant—A person who gives information and wishes to remain anonymous.

Intent—Mental element which directs an event.

Interrogation—A formal and systematic questioning to learn facts and obtain admissions or confessions of wrongful acts from persons.

Interview—An informal questioning to learn facts.

Larceny—The wrongful taking, obtaining, or withholding, by any means, of any money, personal property, or article of value of any kind, from the possession of the true owner or of any other person in custody of the same, with the intent to permanently deprive or defraud another person of the use and benefit of such property.

Latent—Hidden; concealed; as in latent fingerprints.

Libel—Damage done, in writing, to the reputation of a person.

LSD—A synthetic drug that can be swallowed or injected and is habit forming. Can cause panic reactions, continuous flashbacks, psychosis, and impaired coordination.

Malum In Se—An act which is immoral or wrong in itself.

Malum Prohibitum—An act which is prohibited by law.

Manslaughter—The unlawful killing of a human being without malice.

Marijuana—A hallucinogenic drug. Those leaves of the Indian Hemp plant can be smoked, swallowed, or chewed. Can cause psychosis, impaired coordination, and conjunctivitis.

Material Evidence—Is that evidence which bears on the credibility of the evidence in some supporting way.

Mens Rea—A guilty mind; a guilty and wrongful purpose; a criminal intent.

Misdemeanor—A crime of a minor nature.

Morphine—A narcotic drug that is extracted from raw opium. Can be swallowed or injected and is addicting in nature. Can cause death, loss of appetite, constipation, loss of sex drive, and loss of productive labor.

Motive—The reason why a person commits a crime.

Moving Surveillance—Secret observation of persons, either by following on foot or in a vehicle, so as to obtain information.

Murder—The unlawful killing of a human being with malice aforethought. The act is willful, deliberate, and premeditated.

Narcotic—An addictive drug which produces insensibility or a stupor due to its depressant effect on the central nervous system. Opium, morphine, heroin, and cocaine are all legally narcotics.

No-Fault Divorce—The dissolution of a marriage upon showing that the marriage is irretrievably broken or has irreconcilable differences.

Opinion Evidence—Very seldom admissible in evidence except in matters of science, profession, or trade; an expert may be asked for his opinion as to the consequences of a fact already proved in evidence; e.g. handwriting or fingerprint experts.

Opium—A narcotic drug that is extracted from the poppy. Can be smoked, chewed, swallowed, or drunk. An addicting drug. Use of the drug can cause death, loss of appetite, constipation, loss of sex drive, and loss of productive labor.

Oral Evidence—That evidence which is related verbally by the witness.

PCP—A hallucinogenic synthetic drug that can be swallowed or smoked. It produces a floating, euphoric high and can cause convulsions, coma, and even death.

Perjury—The willful and corrupt giving, in any official proceeding and upon a lawful oath or equivalent affirmation, of any false testimony material to the issue or matter of inquiry.

Physical Evidence—Any and all objects, living, liquid, gas, solid, or inanimate, and the relationship between all such objects as they pertain to the crime.

Presumption—An inference as to the existence of one fact from the existence of some other known fact.

Public Law—Concerns the rights and obligations people have to society. Criminal Law is a branch of Public Law.

Pyromaniac—A mentally ill person who sets fires for fun to satisfy a compulsion or to excite sexual stimulation and orgasm; one of the most difficult arsonists to detect because he has no rational motive for setting fires.

Real Evidence—That evidence that is furnished by objects which speak for themselves and require no explanation, merely identification.

Relevancy—As it applies to the law of evidence means the logical relation between the proposed evidence and a fact to be proved.

Robbery—The taking, with intent to steal, of anything of value from the person or in the presence of another against his will, by force and violence or fear of immediate or future injury to his person or property, or to persons or property of a relative, or of anyone in his company at the time of the robbery.

Search—An examination of a person's house or other buildings or premises, or of his person, in order to discover evidence of guilt to be used in the prosecution.

Slander—Damage done, in the form of spoken words, to the reputation of a person.

Surveillance—Secret observation of persons, places, or things in order to obtain information.

Tailing—The act of following a person so as to obtain information.

Theft—The unlawful taking of possessions belonging to another; legally called larceny.

Tort—A private wrong. The affected party has a right to collect money to pay for damages suffered; does not include a breach of contract.

Tranquilizer—Synthetic depressant drug that can be taken orally or injected and is addicting in nature. Can cause death, coma, or kidney failure.

Undercover Operative—Placement of a detective in a role situation where his true identity has been changed and a new one adopted so that he can detect violations, gather evidence, identify persons, and recover stolen items.

Venue—The location where the incident occurred; the place at which a case is tried. Also called *situs delicti.*

Final Examinations

After reading this book, the reader can measure his knowledge of the private detective profession by taking the examination that follows. Note that the initial "T" represents "true" in the tests, and "F" represents "false."

To determine your score, multiply the correct number of true and false answers by one point, multiply the correct number of matching answers by two points, and then total both numbers. This figure represents your final score.

SCORE
100 . . . . PERFECT SCORE
95-99 . . . . EXCELLENT
90-91 . . . . GOOD
85-89 . . . . FAIR
84 & below . . . . NEEDS MORE STUDY

EXAMINATION 1

Circle
Answer

T - F   **1.** The only business a private detective can work for is a detective agency.

T - F   **2.** Detaining a person is considered an arrest.

T - F   **3.** A private detective is not liable for false arrest.

T - F   **4.** A private detective can legally search anyone, at any time.

T - F   **5.** A private detective can use reasonable force if he believes someone intends to do him harm.

T - F   **6.** Written defamation is slander.

T - F   **7.** A person with a criminal record can become a private detective.

T - F   **8.** Generally, hearsay evidence is not admissible in court.

T - F   **9.** A confession is an exception to the hearsay evidence rule.

T - F   **10.** A dying declaration must be written.

T - F   **11.** Evidence is that which supplies proof.

T - F   **12.** Corpus delicti means the body of the crime.

EXAMINATION 2

Circle
Answer

T - F   **1.** A private detective should always disregard small bits of information.

T - F   **2.** The background information form is completed on your initial client contact.

T - F   **3.** Motor vehicle information is found on the state level.

T - F   **4.** Voter registration information is found on the county level.

T - F   **5.** Under the Freedom of Information Act, a private detective can obtain classified information.

T - F   **6.** A professional informer is usually connected with the criminal world.

T - F   **7.** Notes are not as important as your formal report.

T - F   **8.** The formal report can be handwritten.

T - F   **9.** A written statement must be signed by the person who wrote it.

T - F   **10.** Adultery is grounds for an absolute divorce.

T - F   **11.** Opportunity is the only element that must be proven in an adultery case.

T - F   **12.** Background information is not important in a divorce case.

EXAMINATION 3

Circle
Answer

T - F　**1.** An investigation should be objective, thorough, relevant, and accurate.

T - F　**2.** The search of the crime scene should be systematic and thorough.

T - F　**3.** Photography is used to preserve the crime scene.

T - F　**4.** A gun is an immovable type of evidence.

T - F　**5.** Note taking is not necessary when investigating a crime.

T - F　**6.** The two types of evidence that are found at a crime scene are called movable or immovable.

T - F　**7.** Evidence that is sent to the laboratory does not have to be wrapped separately.

T - F　**8.** A laboratory can distinguish between animal and human hair.

T - F　**9.** An elaborate crime lab is needed by the private detective.

T - F　**10.** Interviewing witnesses is a very important part of any investigation.

T - F　**11.** The police are usually the first to investigate major crimes.

T - F　**12.** A private detective should use only that evidence which tends to prove or disprove the matters under investigation.

EXAMINATION 4

T - F   1. Theft is the unlawful taking of possessions belonging to another.

T - F   2. The use of force and/or fear must be present in order to constitute the crime of robbery.

T - F   3. Self-defense is excused from the charge of homicide.

T - F   4. Murder committed while perpetrating a burglary is murder in the first degree.

T - F   5. A killing in the defense of others is murder in the first degree.

T - F   6. Killing in the heat of passion is called manslaughter.

T - F   7. Arson is an act of willful and malicious burning.

T - F   8. A pyromaniac is sometimes called a firebug.

T - F   9. Revenge is a motive of arson.

T - F   10. Manslaughter is the unlawful killing of a human being without malice.

T - F   11. Arson is sometimes committed to hide another crime.

T - F   12. Inflammable liquids are sometimes used to start fires.

EXAMINATION 5

T - F **1.** Surveillance is the secret observation of persons, places, or things.

T - F **2.** Habit forming constitutes a physical dependency caused by drugs.

T - F **3.** Shoplifting is the unlawful taking of merchandise from a retail store.

T - F **4.** An undercover detective should record notes after he has left his assignment for the day.

T - F **5.** Addiction is a mental craving for drugs.

T - F **6.** Heroin is a hallucinogen.

T - F **7.** An undercover detective need not fit into the assignment.

T - F **8.** Opium and heroin are narcotics.

T - F **9.** Reproductions in the third dimension are made chiefly of tire marks, footprints, teeth, and tool marks.

T - F **10.** LSD can cause panic reactions.

T - F **11.** A private detective does not have to perform investigations in a professional, moral, and ethical manner.

T - F **12.** A private detective, when giving testimony in court, should always rely on his memory for facts pertaining to the case in question.

129

EXAMINATION 6

After each item in Column I, indicate the capital letter preceding the item in Column II to which it relates or is identified.

I	II
1. Arrest	**A.** Verbal defamation
2. Libel	**B.** The body of the crime
3. Indirect Evidence	**C.** Written defamation
4. Corpus Delicti	**D.** Taking a person into custody
5. Intent	**E.** Location of the incident
6. Direct Evidence	**F.** Evidence drawn from inferences
7. Duress	**G.** Person who gives or sells information
8. Slander	**H.** Evidence from one's knowledge
9. Informant	**I.** State of mind that directs the criminal act
10. Venue	**J.** Forced or compelled to commit a crime by another
11. Robbery	**K.** Theft from a building
12. Heroin	**L.** Hallucinogen
13. Addiction	**M.** Psychological dependency
14. Shoplifting	**N.** Narcotic
15. LSD	**O.** Theft using force
16. Ethics	**P.** Physical dependency

17. Tort		**Q.**	Principles of professional conduct
18. Burglary		**R.**	Theft from a retail establishment
19. Embezzlement		**S.**	A civil wrong
20. Habit Forming		**T.**	Fraudulent appropriation of entrusted property or money

ANSWERS

Examination 1	Examination 2	Examination 3
1-F	1-F	1-T
2-T	2-T	2-T
3-F	3-T	3-T
4-F	4-T	4-F
5-T	5-F	5-F
6-F	6-T	6-T
7-F	7-F	7-F
8-T	8-F	8-T
9-T	9-T	9-F
10-F	10-T	10-T
11-T	11-F	11-T
12-T	12-F	12-T

Examination 4	Examination 5	Examination 6	
1-T	1-T	1-D	11-O
2-T	2-F	2-C	12-N
3-T	3-T	3-F	13-P
4-T	4-T	4-B	14-R
5-F	5-F	5-I	15-L
6-T	6-F	6-H	16-Q
7-T	7-F	7-J	17-S
8-T	8-T	8-A	18-K
9-T	9-T	9-G	19-T
10-T	10-T	10-E	20-M
11-T	11-F		
12-T	12-F